Walk

in the beautiful

Conwy Valley

By the same Author

Walk in Magnificent Snowdonia

Walk Snowdonia
      Trackways
      Packhorse Trails
      Roman Roads

Walk in the Romantic Vale of Ffestiniog

Walk Snowdonia Peaks

Walk

in the beautiful

Conwy Valley

Ralph Maddern

FOCUS PUBLICATIONS . WINDSOR

© Ralph Maddern

First published in Great Britain 1977
Second edition 1978
Third edition 1979
Fourth edition 1981
Fifth edition 1986
Sixth (revised) edition 1989

Focus Publications Ltd
9 Priors Road
Windsor
Berkshire SL4 4PD.

ISBN 1 872050 00 X

Printed in Great Britain by
Grosvenor Press (Portsmouth) Ltd.

The Walks

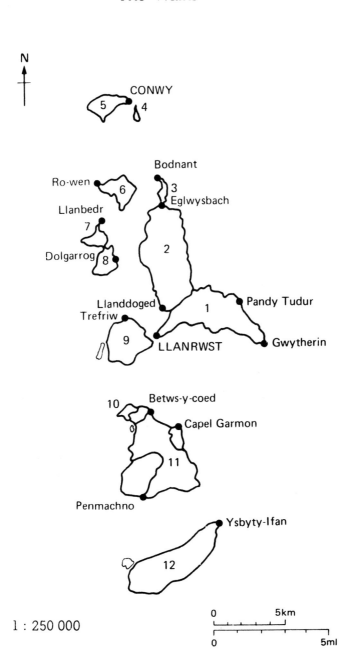

N

CONWY

5   4

Bodnant

Ro-wen   6   3
             Eglwysbach

Llanbedr

7

Dolgarrog   8

                         2

Llanddoged   1   Pandy Tudur
Trefriw
         9   LLANRWST   Gwytherin

                Betws-y-coed
10
             0   Capel Garmon

                11

Penmachno

                Ysbyty-Ifan

                12

1 : 250 000

0   5km

0   5ml

Illustrations

	Page

Illustrations   by   June Jackson

Contents

Compass Bearings

Pedometer Readings

and the Conwy Valley

Accuracy of position and direction is ensured by combining two kinds of measurement: distance registered by a pedometer, and direction recorded by a compass.

A pedometer reading may be taken to be correct to the nearest one-tenth of a kilometre or one hundred metres: 1.7km is within the range 1.65km to 1.75km, 1650 metres to 1750 metres,

A compass bearing of 080° can be accepted as lying within the arc 075° to 085°.

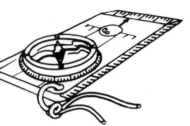

To determine a bearing, hold a hand compass in a horizontal position and allow the needle to steady. Turn the circle graduated in degrees until the N/S marking – 0°/360° to 180° – lies exactly beneath the needle.

If a bearing in this text is to be followed move the base platform until its centre line registers the required reading on the graduated circle.

If the bearing of an object from a position on the ground is required, move the base platform until its centreline is aligned with the object. Read the object's bearing on the graduated circle.

If seeking a bearing from an Ordnance Survey map in order to follow a direction on the ground,
★ place the centre of the graduated circle on the map position from which the bearing is to be taken
★ move the grid lines of the graduated circle to coincide with those of the OS map
★ Align the base platform's centreline on the map with the object whose bearing is required and read the bearing on the graduated circle.

Welsh

Place names in Wales are fascinating because of the descriptions they offer of their locations. That is why interpretations are given where this is possible. Understanding what the name means is often a major clue to knowing the place itself. Pronunciation can be quite difficult for a non-Welsh speaker but is is worth trying to get the right sound. The main sounds, where these differ from English, are set out below.

a	as in *are*
c	always hard as in *car*
Ch	as in the Scottish *loch*
e	"ay" as in *say*
f	as in the English *"v"*
Ff	as in the English *"f"*
g	always hard as in *give*
Ll	place the tongue to form "l" but emit a passage of air through the tongue to merge with the following letter
r	rolled more strongly than in English
Rh	both the "r" and the "h" are pronounced
Th	as in *both*
Dd	also "th" but as in *this*
u	"i" as in *it* or "ee" as in *feet*
w	"oo" as in roost (Llanrwst = Llanroost) – it also works like the English "w"
y	"u" as in *fun* or "ee" as in *feet* or "i" as in *pin* (you have to listen)

J, K, Q, V, X and Z do not appear in Welsh as these sounds are conveyed by other letters or diphthongs.

As with some Welsh poetry the evocative quality in the term *critch-cratch* eludes adequate representation in English. *Critch-cratch* refers to a gate hung in a U or V-shaped enclosure and is, therefore, impassable to stock animals. It is sometimes known as a "kissing gate".

Critch-cratch seems much more illustrative and evocative.

Countryside
COMMISSION

YOUR RIGHTS OF WAY ARE

Public footpaths – on foot only. *Sometimes waymarked in yellow*

Bridleways – on foot, horseback and pedal cycle. *Sometimes waymarked in blue*

Byways (usually old roads), most "Roads Used as Public Paths" and, of course, public roads – all traffic.

Use maps, signs and waymarks. Ordnance Survey Pathfinder and Landranger maps show most public rights of way.

ON RIGHTS OF WAY YOU CAN

Take a pram, pushchair or wheelchair if practicable

Take a dog (on a lead or under close control)

Take a short route round an illegal obstruction or remove it sufficiently to get past.

YOU HAVE A RIGHT TO GO FOR RECREATION TO

Public parks and open spaces – on foot

Most commons near older towns and cities – on foot and sometimes on horseback

Private land where the owner has a formal agreement with the local authority.

IN ADDITION you can *use* by local or established *custom or consent*, but ask for advice if you're unsure:

Many areas of open country like moorland, fell and coastal areas, especially those of the National Trust, and some commons

Some woods and forests, especially those owned by the Forestry Commission

Country Parks and picnic sites

Most beaches

Canal towpaths

Some private paths and tracks.

Consent sometimes extends to riding horses and pedal cycles.

FOR YOUR INFORMATION

County councils and London boroughs maintain and record rights of way, and register commons

Obstructions, dangerous animals, harassment and misleading signs on rights of way are illegal and you should report them to the county council

Paths across fields can be ploughed, but must normally be reinstated within two weeks

Landowners can require you to leave land to which you have no right of access

Motor vehicles are normally permitted only on roads, byways and some "Roads Used as Public Paths"

Follow any local bylaws.

AND, WHEREVER YOU GO, FOLLOW THE COUNTRY CODE

Enjoy the countryside and respect its life and work

Guard against all risk of fire

Fasten all gates

Keep your dogs under close control

Keep to public paths across farmland

Use gates and stiles to cross fences, hedges and walls

Leave livestock, crops and machinery alone

Take your litter home

Help to keep all water clean

Protect wildlife, plants and trees

Take special care on country roads

Make no unnecessary noise.

This Charter is for practical guidance in England and Wales only. Fuller advice is given in a free booklet "Out in the country" available from Countryside Commission Publications Despatch Department, 19–23 Albert Road, Manchester M19 2EQ.

Published with grant aid from the **Countryside** COMMISSION

COMISIWN
Cefn Gwlad

DYMA EICH HAWLIAU TRAMWY

Llwybrau cyhoeddus – ar droed yn unig. *Fe'u dynodir weithiau â'r lliw melyn*

Llwybrau ceffyl – ar droed, ar gefn ceffyl neu feic. *Fe'u dynodir weithiau â'r lliw glas*

Cilffyrdd (hen ffyrdd fel arfer), y mwyafrif o "Ffyrdd a Ddefnyddir fel Llwybrau Cyhoeddus" ac wrth gwrs, ffyrdd cyhoeddus – pob trafnidiaeth. Defnyddiwch fapiau, arwyddion a mynegbyst. *Dangosir y mwyafrif o hawliau tramwy cyhoeddus ar fapiau Pathfinder a Landranger yr Arolwg Ordnans.*

LLE BO HAWLIAU TRAMWY GALLWCH

Fynd â phram, coets gadair neu gadair olwyn os yw'n ymarferol
Fynd â chi (ar dennyn neu dan reolaeth glos)
Gymryd ffordd fer o gwmpas rhwystr anghyfreithlon neu ei symud ddigon i fynd heibio iddo.

MAE GENNYCH HAWL I FYND I HAMDDENA

Mewn parciau cyhoeddus a mannau agored – ar droed
I'r mwyafrif o diroedd comin gerllaw hen drefi a dinasoedd – ar droed ac weithiau ar gefn ceffyl
Ar dir preifat lle mae gan y perchennog gytundeb ffurfiol â'r awdurdod lleol.

YN OGYSTAL gallwch *ddefnyddio* trwy arfer neu ganiatâd *lleol neu sefydlog* ond gofynnwch am gyngor os ydych yn ansicr:

Llawer darn o dir agored fel rhostir, bryniau a'r arfordir, yn enwedig rhai'r Ymddiriedolaeth Genedlaethol a rhai tiroedd comin.
Rhai coedlannau a choedwigoedd, yn enwedig y rhai sy'n eiddo i'r Comisiwn Coedwigaeth
Parciau Gwledig a safleoedd picnic
Mwyafrif ein traethau
Llwybrau ymyl y camlesi
Rhai llwybrau a thraciau preifat
Estynnir caniatâd weithiau i gynnwys mynd ar gefn ceffyl neu feic.

ER GWYBODAETH I CHI

Mae cynghorau sir a bwrdeisdrefi Llundain yn cynnal a chofnodi hawliau tramwy, ac yn cofrestru tir comin
Mae rhwystrau, anifeiliaid peryglus, erledigaeth ac arwyddion camarweiniol yn anghyfreithlon a dylech roi gwybod i'r cyngor sir amdanynt
Gellir aredig llwybrau sy'n croesi caeau, ond rhaid eu hadfer o fewn pythefnos fel arfer
Gall tirfeddiannwyr fynnu eich bod yn gadael tir lle nad oes gennych hawl mynediad
Ni chaniateir moduron fel arfer ond ar ffyrdd, cilffyrdd a rhai "Ffyrdd a Ddefnyddir fel Llwybrau Cyhoeddus"
Parchwch unrhyw is-ddeddfau lleol

A, LLE BYNNAG YR EWCH, DILYNWCH Y RHEOLAU CEFN GWLAD

Mwynhewch y wlad a pharchwch ei bywyd a'i gwaith
Gwyliwch rhag holl beryglon tân
Caewch bob llidiard
Cadwch eich cŵn dan reolaeth glos
Cadwch at lwybrau cyhoeddus wrth groesi tir amaethyddol
Defnyddiwch lidiardau a chamfeydd i groesi ffensys, gwrychoedd a waliau
Gadewch lonydd i anifeiliaid, cnydau a pheiriannau
Ewch â'ch sbwriel adre gyda chi
Helpwch gadw pob dŵr yn lân
Cymerwch ofal o goed, creaduriaid a phlanhigion gwyllt
Byddwch yn ofalus iawn ar ffyrdd gwledig
Peidiwch â chreu sŵn yn ddiangen

Arweiniad ymarferol yw'r canllawiau hyn yng Nghymru a Lloegr yn unig. Ceir cyngor manylach o Swyddfa Cymru, Comisiwn Cefn Gwlad, Tŷ Ladywell, Y Drenewydd, Powys SY16 1RD.

Cyhoeddwyd gyda chymorth ariannol

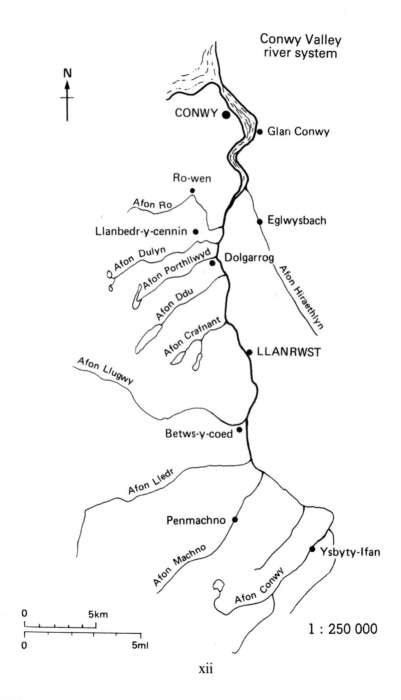

Conwy Valley
river system

N

CONWY
Glan Conwy

Ro-wen
Afon Ro

Eglwysbach

Llanbedr-y-cennin

Afon Dulyn
Afon Porthllwyd
Dolgarrog

Afon Ddu
Afon Hiraethlyn

Afon Crafnant

LLANRWST

Afon Llugwy

Betws-y-coed

Afon Lledr

Penmachno

Ysbyty-Ifan
Afon Machno

Afon Conwy

0 — 5km

0 — 5ml

1 : 250 000

xii

The Conwy and its Valley

Well before the last Ice Age, generous rains falling over Snowdonia began washing a large groove out of the mountains, channelling an escape route to the sea. Then, as the earth's axis tilted, withdrawing the poles from the sun, glaciers continued the process of deepening and widening. When the ice departed, the rains returned to wash down from the mountains vast quantities of alluvium which spread out over the Conwy Valley to make the fine, flat, fertile floor we see today.

The tributary valleys, having had less water to cope with during their equally long lives, have remained steeper and narrower. Here we can take a long step back in time. With less cultivation and settlement there is a greater amount of natural countryside. Up near the source of the Conwy, where countless tributary streams drain moors and mountains, there

13

is a vast expanse of open country; it is an area of bell-heather and cotton grass seldom trodden except by a few sheep and occasional walkers.

Immediately below are a trio which must rank very high in the scale of scenery exhibitors: the Machno, Lledr and Llugwy Valleys. The Machno begins life as a myriad of turbulent streams in the mountains above Ffestiniog, subdues into an orderly flow until it tumbles over waterfalls into the Conwy. Downstream, romantic Fairy Glen whips white water through its narrow gorge towards a confluence with the Lledr, a mountain river that retains an atmosphere of remote originality because of the steepness of its valley and an absence of large settlement. The Llandudno–Ffestiniog railway is this valley's major piece of human engineering. Opened to passenger traffic in 1881 this line runs along most of the Conwy Valley; when it turns up the Lledr it reaches its scenic climax with incomparable views on all sides.

Lower down, the Llugwy's renowned beauty, inspiration to generations of artists, is undiminished by increasing attention from visitors. Walkers should feel assured: the world may come to a few well-publicised spots but once we are away from the tarmac this splendid world is ours.

Further north the two lakes, Crafnant and Geirionydd, give birth to the Afon Crafnant which flows down through Trefriw; the reservoir Eigiau feeds the Porthllwyd providing Dolgarrog with power for its aluminium works; the Dulyn, rising from two small lakes deep in the mountains, drains under the feet of Llanbedr-y-cennin; the Ro issues from the gap where the Romans built their road through the mountains to Caernarfon.

On the eastern side the upland moors lack sufficient height to provide powerful tributaries. But the Hiraethlyn, which flows gently through Eglwysbach and down to the Conwy past the Bodnant Garden, has sculptured a beautiful valley.

The lower Conwy is the area of the river's oldest industries: pearl fishing, boat building and water transport. Carried on at least since Roman times on the stretch between Trefriw and Conwy, pearl fishing was thriving until well into the nineteenth century. A Conwy pearl is said to be among the Crown Jewels having been presented to the Queen of Charles II.

Records of a boat-building industry can be traced back four hundred years. "Katherin of Conwaye" was built at Conwy in 1565, "George of Conway" in 1584. The size of these sixteenth-century craft is not known but "Hopewell", built at Llanrwst in 1756, weighed 25 tons; "Union of Caernarfon", built at Tal-y-cafn in 1789, 35 tons; "Providence", built at Glan Conwy in 1799, 58 tons. Of course, the river level was higher then than it is today: craft were navigable to a point just below Llanrwst where sails and ropes were made.

The outward-bound cargo down-river was usually slate; cargo brought upstream consisted mainly of coal, salt and provisions. The principal port was Trefriw which, in the early nineteenth century, handled about four hundred commercial craft each year. Voyages were not confined to the river. Some Conwy river craft docked along the coast in Mostyn, Flint and other harbours in North Wales; some sailed as far as Chester and Liverpool.

Nothing is left of this industry now but looking at the Conwy after heavy rain we can imagine how it once was when the river was a vital means of transport; and how paddle steamers once docked at Trefriw Quay.

The charm of Llanrwst – centre of the Conwy Valley

Stand on the east bank of the Conwy, facing west to the Snowdon massif, a little downstream from the Llanrwst Bridge. Choose an early morning when the sky is lightening and the mountains still cling to darkness. Feel the timelessness. This view has probably changed very little since William Salesbury, translator of the New Testament into Welsh, resided here in the sixteenth century.

Walk along the bank to the bridge and up to the top of the centre arch. Face the oncoming stream and the dawn. And listen – to the melted snows from Snowdon and the drenching rains from Ffestiniog rippling away at the stones beneath: a sound that was probably familiar to Inigo Jones who is said to have designed this bridge, built in 1636. Thump the parapet and feel the vibration in the structure. Perhaps the bridge's indestructible quality owes something to its capacity to respond to any force applied to it. This is no museum piece, for it handles any form of twentieth-century traffic as easily as it served seventeenth-century carts or Civil War cavalry. Here is a splendid utility and a superb feature combined: Llanrwst's guarantor of identity in past and future ages, its subject for countless paintings in tribute to its uniqueness.

Llan refers to a church and the area associated with it such as a village or town. Many place-names starting with Llan have a saint's name following. *Gwrgwst* (the equivalent of "Firgus" in Gaelic meaning a strong man) was a sixth-century saint whose name has been compressed to Rwst. Hence, *Llanrwst:* the church of *Rwst*.

From its remote past Llanrwst has preserved these words: *Cymru, Lloegr a Llanrwst* – Wales, England and Llanrwst. This saying is said to have originated with the early inhabitants of the district known as *Y Gwylliaid* or Men of the Dusk who refused to recognise any law or authority other than their own. Later, when North Wales was divided among Fifteen Noble Tribes by Nefydd Hardd, Llanrwst was not included, and as it could not by any stretch of the imagination be considered part of England, it came to regard itself as a separate entity.

According to William Williams in *Ancient and Historic Llanrwst*, 1930, Llanrwst's early history was stormy and violent. Tradition links one Llywarch, who was a bard as well as a leader of warriors, with battles fought here about the year 610. In the ninth century Rhodri the Great, King of Wales, divided his kingdom among three of his sons. He left Gwynedd (North Wales) to his eldest son, Anarawd, who reigned from 877 to 913. Dyfed (South Wales) went to Rhodri's second son, Cadell, and Powys to his third son, Merfyn. Three generations later the great-grandsons of the Welsh King fought bloody battles in South Wales and here in the north at Llanrwst.

When Hywel Dda, son of Cadell, died, the northern princes, Ieuaf and Iago, grandsons of Anarawd, invaded South Wales and scored a victory over the southern forces, led by Owain, grandson of Cadell. In retaliation, the southern princes, Dyfnal and Rhodri, brothers of Owain, marched north and met the army of Ieuaf and Iago at Llanrwst in the year 954. Ieuaf and Iago won a narrow victory and followed it by again invading the south in the same year. Again they were victorious, defeating the southern forces under Edwin, another grandson of Cadell.

At the beginning of the fifteenth century Llanrwst was

18

the scene of bitter fighting when the Welsh tried to re-establish their independence under the leadership of Owain Glyndwr. Later in the same century, in 1468, there was complete devastation, including the burning of the church, when the forces of King Edward IV lay waste the habitats of the king's rivals up and down the Conwy Valley.

The last time Llanrwst provided a scene of battle was in the Civil War of the seventeenth century when, as part of Royalist territory, it was an important objective of the Parliamentary army because of its bridge which had been completed six years before the war broke out in 1642. In taking Llanrwst the Parliamentarians were able to sweep on over the bridge in pursuit of their enemies who had sought refuge in the mountains west of the town.

The Conwy was by tradition a frontier river. To the west in the dark forbidding mountains was the Welsh heartland, the refuge for retreating Welsh warriors when under attack from the English. To the east was disputed territory, the area of Welsh sortie and counter-attack, the region of English consolidation. But Llanrwst is a town that the English have never consolidated.

Go to the square which has been the market place of the Conwy Valley for centuries. Nowadays, customers sort over goods that were produced anywhere – such is the nature of the market economy in this age of uniformity and standardisation. But in times past you could buy your needs in this square from commodities produced in the valley. Those were the times of natural conservation and a genuine village economy when producer and consumer often knew each other and chemicals were to do with gunpowder not fertiliser.

Here was where you could get a man or a maid, if you had need of either, at the Ffair Gyflogi, held each May and November. You could walk along a line of strong labourers and demure maids and secure the worker of your choice by pressing a shilling, or sixpence if that was the smallest piece you had, into his or her hand. You had to provide food, of course, and a bed, but you would be well served for sixteen hours a day. Your only other obligation to your employee would be a pittance of pocket money for an outing to town once a week.

This was the Saturday evening outing when unattached men all over the valley put on their best and tramped to the square in freshly polished boots. There they would gather in doorways to discuss prospects for the night's sport. Some would drift into pubs to slake their thirsts and bolster their courage. A jug of bitter did wonders for a shy fellow but he had to weigh the benefit of this indulgence against the censure of a well brought up girl who might consider alcohol not just unseemly but sinful.

At dusk the girls appeared, not now demure but pretending not to notice the tentative challenge from the doorways. They could not appear forward by accepting too easily, but such restraint melted in full darkness when boldness grew from the shadows and fed on slight encouragement.

Then the hounds gave chase. Into the seclusion of Tan yr Eglwys or Tan y graig; or the labyrinth of alleyways where the new library and flats now stand. Or into the open darkness of Denbigh Street. Wherever there was unlit anonymity new love affairs could begin.

Walk 1

Llanrwst – Pandy Tudur – Gwytherin – Llanrwst: 26½km, 16½ml.

Llanrwst – Pandy Tudur: 11km, 6.9ml.

From the Llanrwst PO (00km; elevation 16m, 50ft) walk SE into Denbigh Street, eastward to the Llanddoged Road (0.5km), turn left and take the right fork (0.6km) over a bridge leading to Cae Tyddyn.

Cae is Welsh for field, *tyddyn* is a cottage. *Cae tyddyn* describes a cottage in a field or a small holding. The cottage

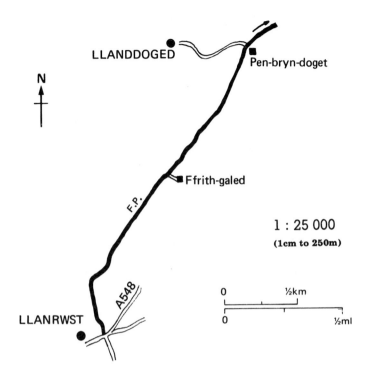

N

LLANDDOGED

Pen-bryn-doget

F.P.

Ffrith-galed

1 : 25 000

(1cm to 250m)

A548

LLANRWST

| 0 | ½km |
| 0 | ½ml |

in the field has long since disappeared and is now replaced by a housing estate!

Follow Cae Tyddyn, compass bearing 050°, to a path which lies between the houses numbered 73/74/76/78 and 94/96. Turn right past house number 94 and continue to a field path.

Follow the path through the first *critch-cratch*, continue under a tunnel of vegetation leading to critch-cratch 2, beyond which there is an open field, where the path divides. Continue up the field, bearing 040°, to critch-cratches 3, 4 and 5.

Ten metres up the lane from critch-cratch 5 turn right to critch-cratch 6 and continue along the hedge, bearing 070°, through an opening to Ffrith-galed (1.9km, 1.2ml; elevation

147m, 450ft). *Ffrith* is an enclosed mountain pasture, *galed* is hard. *Ffrith-galed:* a hard enclosed mountain pasture.

Already in this short distance we are well above the town; for the best view cross the yard to critch-cratch 7 and continue along the hedge to the brow of the hill. From here Llanrwst displays itself as a model spreading north and south by the leisurely meandering Conwy.

Leaving the next critch-cratch veer right to critch-cratch 9, on through a fence opening, along the fence, bearing 040°, and over a stile in the corner of the field. Continue northward to critch-cratches 10 and 11 and on to Pen-bryn-doget (2.9km, 1.8ml; elevation 184m, 560ft). *Pen* means head or brow, *bryn* is a hill, *doget* (or *doged*) refers to a saint. *Pen-bryn-doget:* the brow of Doged's hill. Llanddoged, the church of Doged, is 800m down the hill to the west.

From Pen-bryn-doget turn right and follow the council road for 450m to a farm entrance turning left (030°) to Pant-

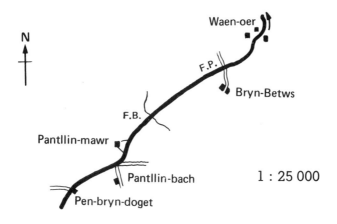

N

Waen-oer

F.P.

Bryn-Betws

F.B.

Pantllin-mawr

Pantllin-bach

1 : 25 000

Pen-bryn-doget

llin-mawr (3.5km, 2.2ml; elevation 194m, 590ft). *Pant* is a hollow, *llin* is flax. *Pantllin:* a flax hollow. *Mawr* is large, *bach* small. Pantllin-bach is 300m to the south of Pantllin-mawr.

The farmhouse at Pantllin-mawr, like many others in the district, dates from the early nineteenth century when larger farmhouses were being built in North Wales following the passing of the Enclosure Acts which drove many poorer farmers from the land and concentrated agriculture into larger units where new methods could be employed to provide food for increasing city populations. An old house, dating back to the seventeenth century, still survives at Pantllin-mawr as does an old bakery near the farmhouse.

Continuing along the drive beyond the yard one arrives at two adjacent gates opening to fields. Take the left gate by the fence and continue to the bottom of the field where there is a footbridge across a stream. Cross the footbridge and continue straight up the hill, on a bearing of 070°, to Waen-oer, avoiding all gates on the right while passing Bryn Betws.

The path passes through the yard at Waen-oer (5.0km, 3.1ml; elevation 238m, 725ft). *Waen* is open land, *oer* cold. *Waen-oer* cold open land. Walk along the drive to a council road, turn right and follow the road E past Ffrithuchaf (6.1km, 3.8ml; elevation 295m, 900ft). *Uchaf* is higher, *isaf* lower. *Ffrithuchaf:* a higher enclosed mountain pasture.

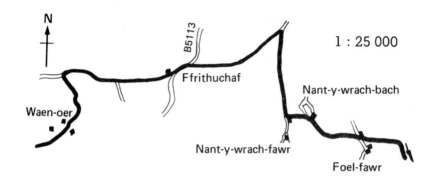

Cross the B5113 to the Llangernyw turnoff, 200m from Ffrithuchaf, continue along the Llangernyw Road for about 750m to a right-turning, a farm road which lies southward to Nant-y-wrach-fawr (7.8km, 4.9ml; elevation 279m, 850ft). *Nant* is a gorge or brook, *fawr* is big, *bach* small. But the meaning of *wrach* is wrapped in mystery: possibly it refers to a watch-place or, more romantically, to a stream where witches dwell.

Before reaching the farmyard turn left, bearing 050°, along the hedge past the house and down to a gate by the stream. Cross the stream and continue diagonally up the field (100°) to Nant-y-wrach-bach. From the yard gate follow the fence path S through a gated opening and on for about 100m to another gated opening on the left; cross the field, bearing 080°, to *Foel-fawr* – big bald top; continue through a gated opening, passing a well on the left, to another gated opening and a hill of rough bracken. The Foel farmhouse is now on the right lower down.

Coming out of the bracken continue along the edge of the field and down to a stream. Walk a short distance upstream until a gate is sighted. Cross the stream at this point and climb up through the gated opening onto wheeltracks. Follow the wheeltracks downhill (S) to a concrete drive which leads up to Fron-deg (9.2km, 5.8ml; elevation 246m, 750ft). *Fron* is a slope, *deg* pleasant. *Fron-deg:* a pleasant slope.

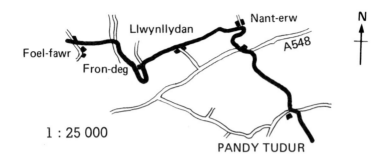

Pass through the yard at Fron-deg to the NE gate and along the contour of a park-like grassy slope to Llwynllydan. *Llwyn* is a grove, *llydan* wide. *Llwynllydan:* a wide grove. Continue along the field path through several gated openings to Nant-erw (bearings 060° to 080°). *Derw* describes oak trees. Nant-derw, shortened to *Nant-erw:* a dale of oaks. Follow the farm road down past Bodnant bungalow (10.3km, 6.4ml; elevation 203m, 620ft), cross the A548 and walk easterly along it for approximately 80m to critch-cratch 12.

Bear 140° over a footbridge which spans the Afon Dyffryn – valley river – and follow the path, veering left then right, up the field, through a gated opening and along a fence to a lane which passes between two houses, Bryn Celyn and Tegfan. Continue down the lane and left over the bridge to the village shop and post office (11.0km, 6.9ml; elevation 222m, 675ft).

Pandy Tudur

Pandy refers to a fulling mill for processing cloth, which suggests that this settlement does not have an ancient origin as do many villages. In the early years of the Industrial Revolution, two natural resources present in remote areas caused an upsurge of activity: soft water and wool. Here, there was a plentiful supply of both: it became a site for cleaning and bleaching wool. At that time the locality was

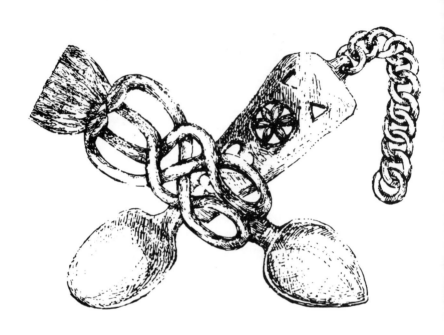

known as *Blaenau Llangernyw* – Upper Llangernyw. Independent status was first achieved under the name *Pandy Budr* – the dirty bleaching place. Dirty because the soft waters of the Afon Derfyn, flowing down across the moors of Maelogan, now a neighbouring farm, carried large quantities of peat which tended to leave the cloth with a brownish tinge.

The peat ended Pandy's career as a cleaning and bleaching place but by the early nineteenth century a settlement was well established with its own Methodist Chapel built in 1770. Craftsmen had settled here including a clockmaker, a candlemaker, a matmaker, a builder, a saddler and, most notable of all, a carver, well known for his carving in most of the local churches, and for his love spoons which were much in demand by wooing young men as tokens of devotion for their beloved.

Sometime in the early nineteenth century these founding fathers, or their immediate descendants, used the Welsh male name, Tudur, to mutate Pandy Budr to Pandy Tudur.

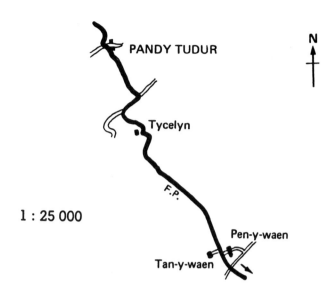

PANDY TUDUR

Tycelyn

F.P.

1 : 25 000

Pen-y-waen

Tan-y-waen

N

The first school, financed by local farmers, was opened in 1845 and it is said that its pupils used the path which is now part of this walk to Gwytherin, coming and going past the mill which was in the centre of the village.

Pandy Tudur – Gwytherin: 3.8km, 2.4ml.

Midway between the Pandy Tudur PO and the bridge turn south to critch-cratch 13, continue to critch-cratch 14 and follow the hedge to a stile at the side of a council road.

Turn right and follow the road for 180m to a left-turning to Tycelyn (11.8km, 7.4ml; elevation 260m, 790ft). *Ty* is a house, *celyn* a holly tree. *Tycelyn:* house of the holly tree.

Pass through the yard to the S gate and follow the wheel-tracks for a little over 200m to a gated opening on the left at the corner of a field. Bear 140° diagonally across the field and continue through three gated openings to an overgrown lane. Follow this lane for 450m between Pen-y-waen and Tan-y-

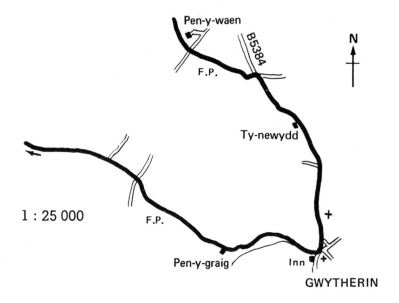

waen to a council road. *Pen-y-waen:* at the top of the waen
(land); *Tan-y-waen:* at the bottom of the waen.

Cross the council road to critch-cratch 15 and continue
through fence openings for about 600m to another council
road. Turn left along this road to the B5384, then right past
Ty Newydd – new house – to Gwytherin (14.9km, 9.3ml;
elevation 246m, 750ft).

Gwytherin

A sixth-century saint, *Gwytherin*, son of Dingad ap
Nudd Hael, founded a church here. On the northern side of
the present churchyard there are four stone slabs, approximately two metres apart and one metre high. The western-
most slab is a memorial to VINNEMAGLI FILI SENE-
MAGLI, buried in the sixth or seventh century. The chur-

chyard gate proclaims the name of St Winifred who established a nunnery here.

Have this village's ancient origins conditioned its shape
and layout? Walking down the hill from Gwytherin's young
neighbour, Pandy Tudur, one can imagine a compact
medieval settlement. Is it true, as is said locally, that
Gwytherin has its own particular Welsh dialect, a product of
hard working, independent-minded people living in a rigor-
ous environment? Why did the pub survive the Methodist
Revivals when the one in Pandy Tudur, and those in other
places, were converted to chapels?

Questions to ponder as one takes refreshment in the
hospitable Gwytherin inn. A challenging climb lies ahead on
the first part of the walk back to Llanrwst.

Gwytherin – Llanrwst: 11.6km, 7¼ml.

From a telephone kiosk marking a point where a stream
from the moor flows east under the B5384 follow wheeltracks
westward along the northern side of the stream, through a
gated opening and onto a stream path which rises 130m
(400ft) in 600m (bearings 320° to 250°) to Pen-y-graig.
Reaching the top of the rise one looks back at Gwytherin,
appreciating why the ancients chose that particular site – beneath the shoulders of protective hills.

At *Pen-y-graig* – top of the rock – pass to the north of
the deserted house through two gated openings and on to
open moorland. From the second gate follow wheeltracks,
bearing 300°, for 350m to a point where the fence veers away
to the right. Continue on 300° for a further 200m to a stile
which is the highest point of the walk at an elevation of
426km (1300ft). Descending, one can enjoy a magnificent
panoramic view of mountains, moorlands and rich lowland
stretching more than 16km (10ml) across the Conwy Valley
to Snowdonia.

Continue to the next fence and on down to critch-
cratch 16 and a council road; along the road, bearing 310°,

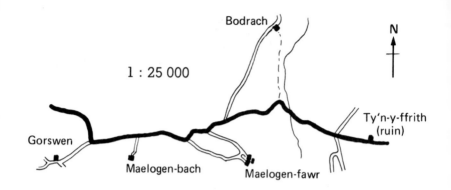

past *Ty'n-y-ffrith* – higher small holding – to a gated opening where the road turns NE and wheeltracks continue west.

Follow the wheeltracks, bearing 290°, down to a bridge which spans the *Afon Derfyn* – boundary river. This track passes between Bodrach to the north and Maelogan-fawr to the south, and joins a council road by a lodge cottage (map ref: 846622; 20.4km, 12.8ml; elevation 362m, 1100ft). Turn right along the council road, bearing 290°, to critch-cratch 17, which is on the right 250m west of *Pen-y-ffridd* – top enclosed pasture. Follow the fence northward through a small wood and two critch-cratches (18 and 19), veering westward north of Gorswen. *Gors* is a bog, *wen* white. *Gorswen:* white bog.

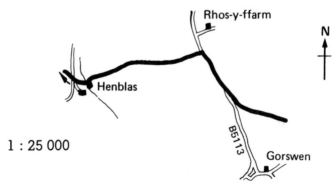

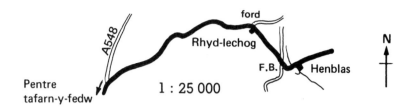

Rejoin the road and continue northward for 350m to critch-cratch 20 which is on the left, south of the entrance to Rhos-y-ffarm. (*Rhos* is a moor or heath). Bear westward along the fence to critch-cratch 21, on down to a footbridge over a stream, then follow the wheeltracks through several gated openings to Henblas (23.1km, 14.6ml; elevation 222m, 675ft).

Hen means old or ancient, *plas* or *blas* is a mansion. *Henblas:* old mansion. During the Wars of the Roses in the fifteenth century, when King Edward IV (1461–83) sent an army to lay waste a large area of North Wales in retaliation for similar destructions by his enemies, an expeditionary commander was received at Henblas where the host, Rhys ap Einion, married to the commander's cousin, offered his guest a harp to play himself to sleep – a favoured method of relaxation. The Welsh tradition of hospitality paid off: Henblas, and its neighbour Brynsyllty, were spared, while Llanrwst and the entire Conwy Valley were consumed by fire and sword in a great orgy of devastation.

Cross the council road to critch-cratch 22 and bear 330° along the stream path to critch-cratch 23; cross the footbridge to critch-cratch 24 and Rhyd-lechog. *Rhyd* describes a ford, *lechog* is stony. *Rhyd-lechog:* a stony ford.

Bear westward along the council road and, with a broad view of the Snowdonian peaks ranged on the horizon ahead, descend to the hamlet of Tafarn-y-fedw (24.7km, 15.4ml; elevation 90m, 275ft). The tavern *(tafarn)* among the birch *(fedw* or *bedw)* was long ago replaced by a chapel, a conversion achieved by one of the Methodist Revivals.

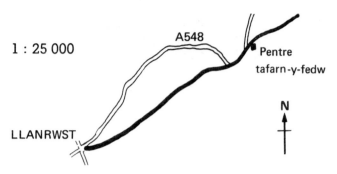

1 : 25 000

A548

Pentre
tafarn-y-fedw

N

LLANRWST

Continue S along the A548 for about 200m to a point where the road veers right and wheeltracks continue on a bearing of 250°, marking out the line of the old Llanrwst road which was used for centuries before motor vehicles demanded gentler grades. It takes a steep plunge down Town Hill, the name Llanrwst gives this incline which rises from the corner of Denbigh Street and Llanddoged Road.

Eglwysbach

It nestles in Cwm Hiraethlyn one of the tributary valleys of the lower Conwy – not far from the main road (A596) but far enough to be able to lead a life of its own. *Cwm* is a valley (usually a higher one), *hiraeth* means longing, *llyn* lake. *Cwm Hiraethlyn:* valley of longing water – an apt and delightful name. *Eglwys* is a church. *Eglwysbach:* little church – no doubt a very much earlier one than the present structure which dates from the sixteenth-century Reformation.

One has a feeling of continuity here: in the hills bisected by a Roman road with its geometric features of constant width and direct alignment; in the church that combines four hundred years of building and re-building from the sixteenth to the nineteenth centuries; in the village smithy where generations of blacksmiths have been shoeing horses since 1628.

Local people speak of "the peace and tranquillity that is a feature of our village". Standing in front of the church, by the Bee Inn, and looking south down the main street, once the scene of colourful fairs, one may well be fortunate enough to hear only the cry of gulls on foraging missions from the coast. Here we are off the beaten tracks, behind one of the Conwy Valley's protective ridges where a community can preserve some of its individuality.

Much of that individuality is concentrated in the village school founded in 1835. In 1985 Ysgol Eglwysbach celebrated 150 years of schooling in the same building. Ysgol Eglwysbach typifies the role which a school plays in concentrating a community's identity and character. It is the object of generosity by those who have things to give or enthusiasm to bestow upon a worthwhile cause. The community is conscious of successive generations being prepared for the future within its environment, and thereby feels assured of its own continuity. A school poses to a community the question of purpose. In Eglwysbach this is related to carrying forward a specific Welshness in the community's heritage which is aided by public awareness of the school's history, researched and written by its present headteacher. It is mainly through its school that Eglwysbach is assimilating culturally different newcomers into its tradition, a process that is possible because successive headteachers and staff have been able to enlist the community's support and co-operation.

Walk 2

Eglwysbach – Llanddoged – Eglwysbach: 22.1km, 13.8ml.

Eglwysbach – Llanddoged: 11.2km, 7ml.

From the Bee Inn (00km; elevation 39m, 120ft) walk south along the main street for 70m and turn left along a council road which rises steeply out of the village, winding easterly and south-easterly. At 1.7km (1.1ml), opposite a deserted farm cottage, *Cefn-gwyn* – white ridge – (map ref: 817701; elevation 229m, 700ft), turn right through a gated

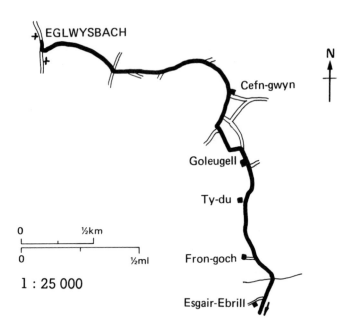

opening onto a field path, bearing 200°, to a stile by a council road. Continue S along the road for 100m to a turning-left onto a farm road which leads to Goleugell. *Goleu* is light; *gell* or *celli*, is a grove. *Goleugell:* a light grove. Follow the farm road southward to Ty-du (2.6km, 1.6ml). *Du* is black. *Ty-du:* black house.

After crossing the cattle grid take the field path to the ruin of Fron-goch. *Bron*, or *fron*, means breast; *coch*, or *goch*, is red. *Fron-goch:* red breast. Continue to a stream crossing where the path veers right to Esgair-Ebrill (3.3km, 2.1ml). *Esgair* is a bank, *Ebrill* April. *Esgair-Ebrill:* April bank.

Pass to the east of the house through gated openings then continue to the next gated opening 200m further on.

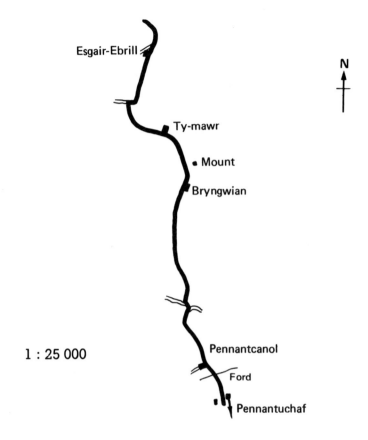

Esgair-Ebrill

N

Ty-mawr

Mount

Bryngwian

1 : 25 000

Pennantcanol

Ford

Pennantuchaf

Keep left round the edge of the field to another gated opening, turn left along wheeltracks and continue S to *Ty-mawr* – big house. This is the high eastern ridge of the Conwy Valley; the higher ground to the east marks the summits of Mynydd (mountain) Esgair-Ebrill and Mynydd Ty-mawr. To the west is a magnificent panoramic expanse of the Conwy Valley and Snowdonia.

Continue south-easterly along the farm road through park-like countryside, passing the farmhouse Mount on the left, to Bryngwian (4.6km, 2.9ml; elevation 262m, 800ft). *Bryn* is a hill; *gwian, gwaun* or *gweun*, is moorland. *Bryngwian:* moorland hill.

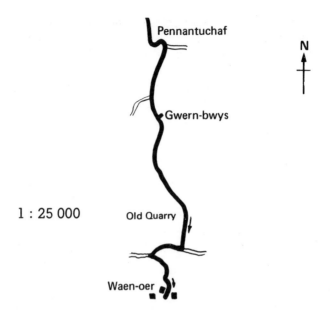

1 : 25 000

The track now bears SW and S to a council road (5.5km, 3.4ml). Follow the road up the hill SE for 100m to wheeltracks which bear S and SE to *Pennantcanol* – the middle pennant – beyond which is a ford through a mountain stream: headwaters of the Afon Hiraethlyn gushing cold and fresh from the mountain at the start of its journey down to Eglwysbach, the Conwy and the sea.

From the ford continue S to *Pennantuchaf* – top pennant – (6.3km, 4ml). (The lowest of the three Pennant farmhouses is about 1.5km NW.) Follow the wheeltracks up the hill veering left then right to a council road. Turn right along the road to face another magnificent view SW across the Conwy Valley.

Continue along the road for about 400m to a farm road on the left which leads to Gwern-bwys (7.1km, 4.4ml). *Gwern* is a swamp; *bwys* or *pwys*, means pressing on. *Gwern-bwys:* pressing on a swamp. The aptness of this name may be judged lower down when crossing a boundary field.

Leaving Gwern-bwys follow wheeltracks to the right through two gated openings, then continue along a hedge on the left for about 150m to two field gates. From the southern gate cross the field, bearing 160°, through a fence opening to an old slate quarry and a deserted house, SE of the quarry.

Follow the wheeltracks southward to a council road, turn right (W) and continue along the farm road for 200m where a left-turning leads to *Waen-oer* – cold land – (8.8km, 5.5ml).

Through the farmyard to the southern gate, SW across fields via gated openings to the farm boundary, uphill along the hedge to the top of the hill; one has a splendid view of Moel-siabod (938m, 2860ft) on a bearing of 240°. Standing apart from its neighbouring peaks, Siabod is the eternal Snowdonia weather beacon, revealing its scalp when all is clear.

Passing Bryn Betws on the left continue by the hedge down to a footbridge (9.8km) at the bottom of the hill, up the field to Pantllin-mawr, along the farm drive to a council road (10.2km). Turn right (W) to Llanddoged (11.2km, 7ml; elevation 147m, 450ft).

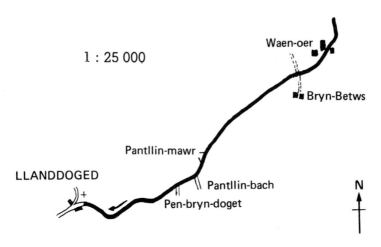

1 : 25 000

Waen-oer

Bryn-Betws

Pantllin-mawr

LLANDDOGED

Pantllin-bach

Pen-bryn-doget

N

Llanddoged

The genesis of Llanddoged is contained in four buildings: the church, enclosed behind its circular wall and its yew trees; *Ty'n Llan* – house in the village – opposite the church on the south side; *Gegin-wen* – white kitchen – next to Ty'n Llan; and *Pen Llan* – top of the village – in front of the church and, as the name suggests, at the top of the descent into the valley below. It is recorded that there are forty springs "within a bow shot" of these houses, including Saint Doged's well which is about 50m north of the church. Saints were practical men: they always set themselves up where there was an unfailing supply of fresh water which was a necessary element in baptism as well as being the most vital sustenance for life.

Standing in the midst of this nucleus one may visualise the essential function of Llanddoged any time after the fourteenth century when the church was founded, though the present structure with its incongruous brick chimney, dates from only 1859. The journey from the coast by horse or coach could be long and uncomfortable and an overnight stop, or at least some congenial refreshment, before descending into the valley, was most desirable. Such was the briskness of the trade that two inns, Ty'n Llan and Pen Llan, were required as well as a cafe in the form of Gegin-wen.

The story is told of one rector – he earned his living by farming – who would go to both inns and the cafe in order to win recruits to his service. Being companionable folk the clients were mostly compliant, the church was only a short distance across the lane and they wanted to give the rector – a local man – his due. But as sermon time approached the worthy rector would see his flock retreat towards Ty'n Llan, Gegin-wen and Pen Llan. Undaunted, he would quickly suspend proceedings, join his errant congregation and carry on his service as best he could in the public houses.

Ty'n Llan became a farmhouse some time towards the end of the nineteenth century, perhaps partly due to the Methodist Revivals and partly because improving transport rendered it redundant. No-one knows when Gegin-wen, which is probably the oldest building in the village, ceased its traditional role. But Pen Llan survived as an inn until the Second World War when faster vehicles and smoother roads finally brought the era of old Llanddoged to an end.

Llanddoged – Eglwysbach: 10.9km, 6.8ml.

From the Llanddoged PO (11.2km, 7ml) walk 80m W past Ty'n Llan and Gegin-wen, turn right in front of the church and follow the village road past Pen Llan, taking the left fork at 11.7km, to a corner 100m further on (map ref: 804640) and critch-cratch 1.

Continue along the hedge for 30m to critch-cratch 2, diagonally across a field to critch-cratch 3 and veer right to a fence opening. Follow the hedge left to a gated opening and take the path across the field to *Parc* – Park (12.6km, 7.9ml).

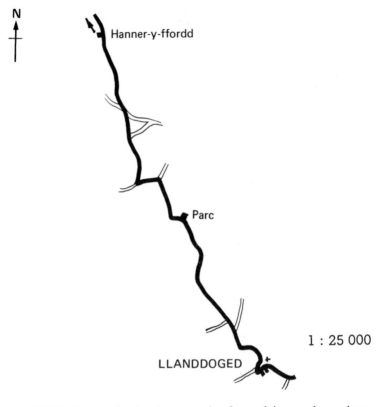

N

Hanner-y-ffordd

Parc

1 : 25 000

LLANDDOGED

Walk alongside the barn to the farm drive and continue down to a council road (13.2km). Turn right and follow the road northward for 400m to a bridge and critch-cratch 4. Continue N along the hedge to critch-cratch 5 (13.7km). Avoiding a left fork follow the council road to Hanner-y-ffordd. *Hanner* means half, *ffordd* way. *Hanner-y-ffordd:* halfway – between Llanrwst and Eglwysbach; and one may observe in the buildings of this farmhouse the aspect of a one-time coaching stop.

Continue along the road for a further 500m to critch-cratch 6 (14.7km), then descend W along a hedge to critch-cratch 7 and Rhiw-dafnau. *Rhiw* refers to a hill, *dafnau* means drops. *Rhiw-dafnau:* drops from the hill. Walk round the north side of the barn to a stile by the farm drive which

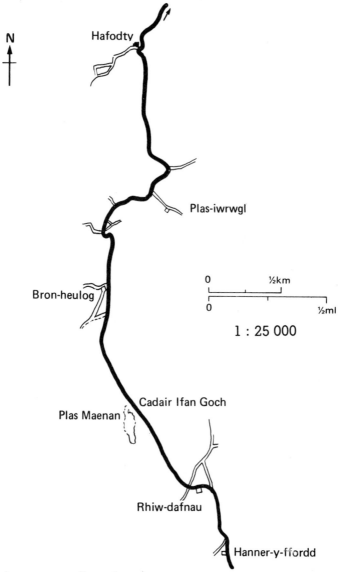

N

Hafodty

Plas-iwrwgl

Bron-heulog

0   ½km

0   ½ml

1 : 25 000

Cadair Ifan Goch

Plas Maenan

Rhiw-dafnau

Hanner-y-ffordd

leads to a council road.

Cross the road to a path by the chapel, bear W for 50m then follow the wheeltracks, bearing 340° to 310°, to Cadair

Ifan Goch (15.8km, 9.9ml; elevation 150m, 550ft). *Cadair* means chair, *coch* red. *Cadair Ifan Goch:* Chair of Ifan the Red. Giants sometimes appear as leading characters in Welsh legends. In one such legend, Ifan, a red giant, sits on this elevated position, bathing his feet in the soothing waters of the Conwy, contemplating what to do with this beautiful valley. So far as is known he is still contemplating.

Bearings: Dolgarrog Aluminium Works 300°; Plas Maenan 257°; Trefriw 200°; Maenan Abbey 183°.

Retrace 100m to the path, bear 340° and follow the path to the cottage Bron-heulog (17.1km, 10.7ml). *Bron* refers to a slope, *heulog* is sunny. *Bron-heulog:* sunny slope.

Follow the wheeltracks round an S-bend and take the northward right fork which joins a narrow council road bearing 040°. Continue along this road past *Plas-iwrwgl* – ivy palace – to the next fork (18.1km). Take the road left, bearing 330°, then N, to critch-cratch 8 which is opposite Hafodty (19.1km, 12ml). *Haf* is summer, *hafod* summer dwelling – to which grazing animals would be moved from winter pasture lower down. *Hafodty:* summer house.

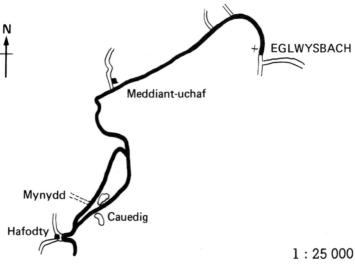

1 : 25 000

Bear E through the woods, veering left then right, to the two small lakes of Mynydd Cauedig. *Mynydd* is highland, *Cauedig* enclosed. *Mynydd Cauedig:* enclosed highland. Pass between the lakes and follow the path round the hill to the NE.

For an alternative route bear N from the woods opposite Hafodty then 040°, past the northern of the two lakes, through a fence opening and directly up the hill where there is a view NE across the valley of Eglwysbach–Cwm Hiraethlyn. From the top of the hill follow wheeltracks which wind down to a gated opening and a farm road.

Bear NW and N to a council road, then NE and E to Meddiant-uchaf (20.7km, 13ml; elevation 189m, 575ft). *Meddiant* means possession, *uchaf* highest. *Meddiant-uchaf:* highest possession. Walk through the farmyard, bearing 070°/060°, to wheeltracks which lead down the hill to the ruin of *Llety* – lodge. We are now on a Roman road, a green glade that becomes a rocky path and is uniform in width as it descends, on a bearing of 060°, to a footbridge (21.7km) spanning the Afon Hiraethlyn. A few hundred metres further on is our starting point in Eglwysbach.

Walk 3

Eglwysbach – Bodnant Garden – Eglwysbach: 5.4km, 3.4ml.

From the Bee Inn (00km) follow the council road north for 400m to a corner where the road turns right and wheeltracks continue north. Follow the wheeltracks for a further 200m to a stile. Continue N, with the hedge on the right, to critch-cratch 1 (0.9km) and further along the hedge to critch-cratch 2 (1.0km) and critch-cratch 3 (1.2km). Turn right along the council road, passing *Gwyndy* – white house – on the left, through the hamlet of Graig (1.8km), then N and NW to the Bodnant Garden (2.7km, 1.7ml).

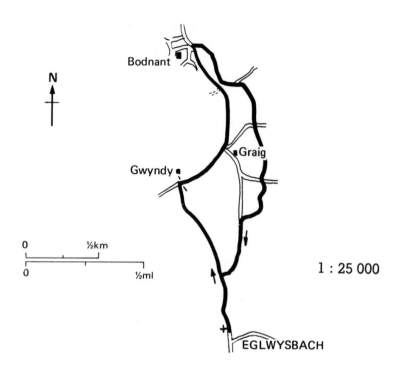

N

Bodnant

Graig

Gwyndy

0   ½km

0   ½ml

1 : 25 000

EGLWYSBACH

The Bodnant Garden is a laboratory of the plant world; a
crucible for propagation and hybridisation; a product of dar-
ing adventure in quest for perfection; a conservatory of rare
species; a remarkable example of consistent philosophy
thoughtfully pursued over successive generations.

In the early years of the twentieth century, collecting
expeditions departed to China, returning with or sending
back plants and seeds that provided the basis for future work
at Bodnant, which dates from 1875 when Henry Pochin, the
first Lord Aberconwy, bought the house and estate facing
magnificent views south-west to Snowdonia. Bodnant has
been developed in accordance with the principle that what
grows well in a garden should be extensively planted in that
garden. Hence, we see displayed not a botanical collection,

but a wide range of interesting and beautiful plants suited to the climate and soil of this corner of the Conwy Valley; set out so that each plant enhances the effect of others and contributes to the general beauty of the garden.

We can appreciate impressive displays of rhododendron, magnolia, camellia, and very many other varieties arranged with an ingenuity redolent of fine art.

The tradition of natural heritage conservation began with hybridisation of plants collected in China. A store of expertise has been built up, backed by purpose-built equipment specifically designed at Bodnant to serve its basic purpose of safeguarding the future of the plant world.

A further accomplishment is the judicious use of commercialisation: meeting a public demand for plants – at the Bodnant Garden Nursery – thereby generating resources for further conservation.

The National Trust has the garden in its care and opens it to the public from 1st April (or Easter) to 31st October.

Leaving the garden entrance walk to the gate in the east corner of the car park, then SE for 100m to a fence opening and 160° across a field to a gated opening by a council road (3.2km). Cross the road to a gated opening and follow wheeltracks up the hill for 200m, then S across a field to a chapel (3.6km). Continue S up the road for 30m to critch-cratch 4, then 160° to critch-cratch 5 and S across a field to critchcratch 6 (4.0km).

Cross the road to critch-cratch 7 and continue to critchcratches 8 and 9 (4.1km). Keeping left round the edge of the field continue to critch-cratch 10 (4.3km) and along the fence to critch-cratch 11. Turn left and follow the council road to Eglwysbach.

Conwy

Here is a rare treasure – a town that is a monument to much of Anglo-Welsh history. One cannot be in Conwy for very long before sensing that great and important events happened here. There is its location at the wide estuary of the Conwy river, a position that is central to the whole region and commands every approach – from the sea, the valley, the mountains. This must have been the assessment of King Edward I who ordered the castle to be built in 1283 to consolidate English power in North Wales following the defeat of the Welsh under Prince Llywelyn. Standing high on its rock foundation it certainly gives the impression of an embattled fortress which it was. The king was himself besieged here with a small force when the Welsh counter-attacked under Madog in 1294–5. But the castle held firm – probably its most crucial test – and the Welsh were forced to retreat.

In 1401, during the revolt led by Owain Glyndwr, Welsh insurrectionists captured the castle by launching a surprise attack while the garrison was attending Good Friday service in the parish church. The Welsh held out for four weeks before surrendering on terms.

During the seventeenth-century Civil War the castle was the Royalist headquarters for North Wales and many of the local gentry used it as a depository for their valuables. John Williams, Archbishop of York and a keen supporter of King Charles I, was in command but the governor was Sir John Owen. The governor eventually ousted the archbishop who retreated to his house at Penrhyn, near Bangor. As the Parliamentary army under General Mytton approached North Wales from Chester the archbishop decided to change sides. He returned to Conwy, took part in the assault over the south wall, and while the castle was under siege, preached in the

parish church to the text: "Blessed be the Lord my strength, which teacheth my hands to war, and my fingers to fight." The castle fell to the Parliamentary army in November 1646. This was its last battle.

The town walls, built at the same time as the castle (1283–8), are generally about 1.5m thick and 5m above the inner ground level. They enclose a quadrilateral of land which could guarantee survival in a medieval siege. The most important gate is Porth-uchaf (Upper Gate Street) in the western wall. Two other main gates are Porth-isaf (High Street) in the eastern wall facing the Conwy river, and Porth-y-felin (Rose Hill Street) in the southern wall. Two smaller gates are Porth-bach in the eastern wall near the castle and Porth-yr-Aden in the spur wall north of the quay.

Within the walls the parish church of St Mary occupies a central position on the site of, and incorporating part of, the structure of a Cistercian Abbey built at the end of the twelfth century. After the English conquest, when Edward I wanted to establish the castle and borough of Conwy, the monks were moved seven miles upstream to Maenan where they founded Maenan Abbey.

Conwy contains a number of Tudor town houses, much restored but giving some idea of what the town might have been like approximately four hundred years ago. They are:

Aberconwy, at the corner of Castle and High Streets, the town's oldest house dating from the fifteenth century;

Plas-mawr (1576–95) in High Street;

Number 22 High Street (16thC) separated from Plas-mawr by a narrow passageway;

Parlwr-mawr (late 16thC) on the north side of Chapel Street;

Old College House (early 16thC) on the west side of Castle Street;

Plas-coch (16thC), Lancaster Square, now incorporating the Bull Inn;

Number 11 Castle Street (1589).

Walk 4

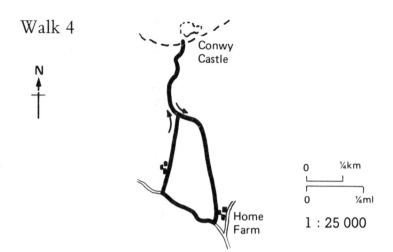

Conwy – Home Farm – Conwy: 3.2km, 2ml.

Down Castle Street past the castle, under the arch (00km) and southward along the Llanrwst Road for 100m to critch-cratch 1 on the left. Climb the hill to a stile and follow the path SW and S along the edge of the woods to critch-cratch 2 (0.5km, 0.3ml; elevation 84m, 275ft). In this short distance we are well above the town and out into the country-side.

Continue SE along the hedge on the right for 200m to a stile, then southward over six more stiles to a council road (1.5km), passing the buildings of Home Farm on the left.

Turn right and continue W/NW up the council road for 400m to a gated opening on the right. Follow the wheeltracks N/NE passing an aerial and farm buildings to critch-cratch 3 (elevation 107m, 350ft). Descending along the wheeltracks one may have clear views of Conwy Mountain (NW), the Great Orme and Conwy Castle (N).

Continue northward to join the outward-bound path (2.5km), then NW and N down to Conwy.

Walk 5

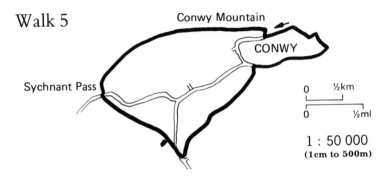

Conwy – Conwy Mountain – Sychnant Pass – Conwy: 8.8km, 5.5ml.

From Lancaster Square (00km) walk NW along the A55, turn left across a railway bridge (0.3km) and right along Cadnant Park Road which veers left to Mountain Road (0.6km).

After passing house number 18 (0.8km) turn right from Mountain Road up the hill to the ridge and continue westward, as splendid views unfold on all sides, to the summit (2.5km, 1.6ml; elevation 246m, 809ft). This may be a small mountain compared with the Snowdonia peaks to the southwest but it is large enough to provide a walker with almost aerial views of the entire Conwy estuary region, a feature that was used by the Romans who built a fortress, Castell Caer Leion, just behind the summit. To the NW is an extensive sea-view between Puffin Island, off Anglesey, and the Great Orme (N). Llandudno bears 030°, Deganwy 060°, Tywyn 080°, Llandudno Junction 100°, Conwy Castle 105°, Glan Conwy 120°, Upper Conwy Valley 180°.

Descend W and SW from the summit to wheeltracks and continue W/SW to Sychnant Pass (4.3km, 2.7ml; elevation 122m, 400ft). *Sych* means dry, *nant* is a gorge. *Sychnant:* dry gorge.

Cross the road and follow the path SE to the cottage *Pen-y-bwlch* – top of the pass – and on down to a council road (5.8km, 3.6ml). Continue SE along the road for about 100m, turn left (NE) through two critch-cratches by a cottage to critch-cratch 3, N to a fence gate (6.1km) and NE, passing

50

Coed Hendre – Hendre Wood – on the right, to critch-cratch 4 (6.6km, 4.1ml). Turn right and follow the drive E through Oakwood Park to a council road. Cross the road to critch-cratch 5 and continue NE to critch-cratch 6, turn left and bear N over a stile to critch-cratch 7 by the council road (7.6km, 4.8ml). Turn right and continue E along the road to Conwy.

Ro–wen

Ro-wen is 7km (4½ml) south of Conwy situated just behind a lower ridge of the Conwy Valley in its own very pleasant cwm. It marks the site of a Roman staging post on the road from Canovium (Caerhun) to Segontium (Caernarfon). From Ro-wen the old Roman road rises steeply westward to *Bwlch-y-Ddeufaen* – gap of the two stones – before descending SW to the straits. About 2km above the village on the northern side of the road is **Maen-y-Bardd** (map ref: 741718) an ancient burial chamber. One sixteenth-century house of note is **Llannerch y-felin** (map ref: 759722).

In its contemporary life Ro-wen is noted for its immaculate appearance – winner of the best kept village award.

Walk 6

Ro-wen – Caerhun (Canovium) – Tal-y-cafn – Ro-wen: 9.4km, 5.9ml.

From the Ty Gwyn public house (00km, elevation 24m, 80ft) walk 30m E along the village road, turn right across the footbridge spanning the Afon Ro and continue SW through a gated opening and along wheeltracks to the farm buildings of Glasgoed (0.4km). *Glas* is green; *coed*, or *goed*, means trees. *Glasgoed:* green trees. Turn left and continue E across the field, then S, following the course of the Afon Ro to critch-cratch 1 (0.9km). Cross the river and the council road, by the

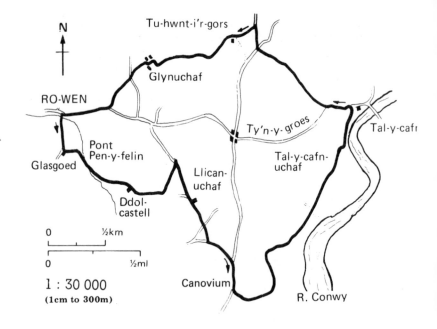

Pont Pen-y-felin – top of the mill bridge – a modernised seventeenth-century bridge, to critch-cratch 2 and continue S/SE to Ddol-castell (1.2km). *Dol*, or *ddol*, is meadow; *castell* means castle. *Ddol-castell:* castle meadow. Walk to the north of the house, through the yard, and continue for 100m along wheeltracks before turning left up the field.

Continue E to a stile, then NE along a hedge and on to a farm road (1.9km). Turn right and follow the road southward past Cefn-isaf and Llican-uchaf to a council road (2.3km). Cross the road and continue S through a field to a stile (2.5km), turn left and follow the road SE to the B5106 opposite Caerhun Hall (2.9km). Turn right along the B5106 to a turning left which leads to St Mary's church Caerhun (3.7km, 2.3ml; elevation 18m, 60ft).

The church occupies the NE quarter of the ancient Roman fort of Canovium, built in the second half of the first century – by Agricola, it is thought, during his campaign of 78.

Canovium remained fully garrisoned for about forty years until Hadrian's reign when, in 121–2, there was a northward movement of troops to build and garrison the Roman Wall. The fort may be observed as an embanked square rising about 1.5m above field level. To the east, between the fort and the River Conwy, are the remains of the Roman baths.

From critch-cratch 3, opposite the church, follow the fence on the right N to critch-cratch 4 (4.0km), bear NE along the hedge to critch-cratch 5, continue alongside the fence to stiles at 4.5km and 4.8km, and on through woods, Coed yr Arw, to another stile at 5.0km. The path now veers to the right along the edge of a field and on to Tal-y-cafn-uchaf (5.2km). Continue through the farmyard and along the drive to the B5279 (5.8km, 3.6ml).

To the right is the Ferry Inn, so-called because a ferry was operated across the river at this point for at least six hundred years until the Tal-y-cafn bridge was opened in 1897. It was a safer crossing than at the mouth of the river and travellers using it could then continue through Ty'n-y-groes and Ro-wen and along the route of the Roman road over the mountains.

Turn left and continue W along the B5279 for 250m to a stile on the right. Bear NW over two fence stiles, through two gated openings, and over two more fence stiles, to the B5106 (6.9km). Continue N along the B5106 for 200m to a fence stile on the left where the path leads across a field to *Tu-hwnt-i'r-gors* – the house beyond the swamp (7.3km, 4.6ml). Pass between the buildings to a field gate opening, then W through a hedge opening into the next field on the right. Follow the hedge on the left to a stile, then bear SW across a field to a corner of the hedge on the right. Follow the hedge round to W, continue into the next field and walk to the right round the edge of the field to a gated opening. Follow wheel-tracks up the hill through gated openings to Glynuchaf (8.3km).

Continue down the farm drive, across a council road to a stile, and follow the fence SW to another council road (9.0km). Turn right and continue down the hill to Ro-wen.

Llanbedr-y-cennin

Llanbedr is 3–4km (2–2½ml) south of Ro-wen, depending upon which route you take. Its elevation is three times that of its neighbour though it is half Ro-wen's distance from the Conwy. This is because it rests upon a lower limb of Pen-y-gaer, that high dome which dominates the entire landscape. A strategic location never escaped the notice of the Romans. *Gaer* refers to a fort. *Pen-y-gaer:* top of the fort, or top fort (elevation 380m, 1247ft). From this mountain stronghold, where remains of Roman settlement and fortification may be observed, the whole of the lower Conwy Valley could be clearly surveyed, especially the river estuary where marauding bands from across the Irish Sea would sometimes appear in flotillas of black coracles. The intention of the Irish raiders was to sweep up the river on a high tide and pillage local settlements. Pen-y-gaer could ensure that the invaders were met in good time.

Llanbedr refers, of course, to the church and village of St Pedr (or Peter). The church dates from the thirteenth century and incorporates additions and restorations carried out in each of the following centuries. It was extensively restored in 1842. *Cennin* describes leeks. Therefore, *Llanbedr-y-cennin:* St Pedr's village of leeks; which suggests a distinctly agricultural notoriety that the village supported well into the twentieth century, for Llanbedr used to give the signal for one of the most significant events in the Conwy Valley's calendar – the putting in of the cows. This was the Llanbedr fair, or *Ffair Lambed*, as it was popularly known, held each year in October. Centred round the Bull Inn, and filling most of the public space in the village, it was a very colourful occasion. With Ffair Lambed it was said that winter had begun.

Llanbedr, a village of character, was naturally attractive to artists, as it still is.

Walk 7

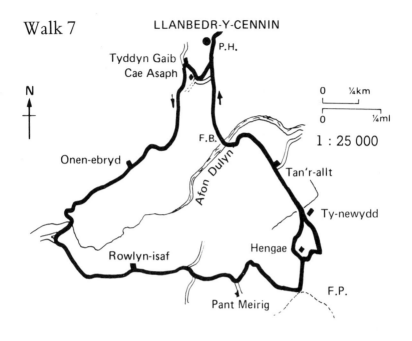

Llanbedr – upper Dulyn – west ridge –
– Llanbedr: 7.4km, 4.6ml.

From the Bull Inn (00km, elevation 74m, 225ft) walk W up the hill along the council road for 100m, fork left by the house Pen-y-graig, and continue for a further 150m to a fork right. Follow this path up the hill for 100m, turn right through a gated opening, and continue to Cae Asaph. *Cae* is a field, *Asaph* is a saint's name. *Cae Asaph:* the field of Asaph. Pass through the farmyard and continue to the right along wheel-tracks past the house to a gated opening by Tyddyn Gaib (0.7km). *Gaib* refers to a pick. *Tyddyn Gaib:* small holding of the pick – a name that says much about the experience of early cultivators on this holding.

From the gate turn left along wheeltracks and continue to the ruined eighteenth-century farmhouse Onen-ebryd (1.5km, 1ml; elevation 286m, 875ft). *Onen* is an ash tree, *pryd* beauty. *Onen-ebryd:* the beautiful ash. With one's back

55

to the ruin the view, at least, offers beauty. South across the tributary valley is Rowlyn-isaf, the next farmhouse on the walk.

Continue along the mountain track to a gated opening (1.8km), turn left along the wall to a gate (2.0km), bear S for about 70m, then W, and follow the high bank of the Afon Dulyn to a fence where the path winds down to the stream. Cross the stream and follow wheeltracks up the hill to a field gate (2.4km), continue to a farm road, turn left and follow the road SE and E to Rowlyn-isaf (3.1km, 1.9ml). Conwy and Llandudno bear 020°, Old Colwyn and Llanelian-yn-Rhos 037°: from this point the coastal towns look quite insignificant against the expanse of valley and sea.

Continue E along the road for 400m, take a right fork for 100m, then a left fork and follow the farm road past *Cae Fadog* (Madoc's field), Pant Meurig (Meurig's hollow), and eastward down the hill past *Llidiard Fadog* (Madoc's gate). Avoid all left-turnings from the path until a stile on the right is sighted (4.8km, 3ml). Here the path touches the route of Walk 8. Continue beyond this style for about 10m to a narrow path on the left, winding northward through the woods, to Hengae (5.1km). *Hen* is old; *cae*, or *gae*, is field. *Hengae:* old field.

From the northern yard gate at Hengae continue (030°) for 100m to a hedge opening, turn left (340°) to a stile and right (020°) down the field to a fence opening by Ty-newydd. Cross the stream and continue (340°) over three stiles to Tan'r-allt (5.8km, 3.6ml; elevation 57m, 175ft). *Tan* means under, *allt* is a hillside. *Tan'r-allt:* under the hillside.

Continue up the council road for about 400m to a point 10m beyond an S-bend and take a path on the right bearing SW into the woods. Follow the path down to a footbridge which spans the Afon Dulyn, and northward, avoiding a stile on the right. Join a path from Pennant on the left and continue northward to the outward-bound path (7.0km), and then down to Llanbedr.

Dolgarrog

This twentieth-century industrial village is strung out along the B5106 between two mountain streams, the Afon Porthllwyd, 2km (1¼ml) south of Llanbedr, and the Afon Ddu 1.5km further south. There was once a hamlet, centuries old, where the Afon Ddu flows under the road and down to the Conwy, but it did not provide a centre, or nucleus, for the later development; it is now simply the southern end of rows of houses. At the northern end is the aluminium works which was sited here in 1907 to use the plentiful supply of water in the mountains for the generation of hydro-electric power.

Like many industrial communities Dolgarrog marks its high point of experience in terms of disaster. On the night of 2nd November 1925 the Eigiau dam, 6km (4ml) in the mountains to the west, burst through its weir and the resulting torrent carried everything before it as it swept down the Porthllwyd Valley. Water swirled into the aluminium works "where 20 furnaces exploded, killing or seriously injuring some workers" (North Wales Weekly News, October 23, 1975). Sixteen lives were lost and the debris, in the form of huge boulders, still lies at the northern end of the village alongside the Conwy road – a permanent memorial to the 1925 disaster.

Walk 8

Dolgarrog – Ardda – Dolgarrog: 7.4km, 4.6ml.

From the Dolgarrog PO, opposite the aluminium works, (00km; elevation 15m, 50ft) walk northward along the B5106 for 400m – passing "disaster debris" on the left – to a lane 50m beyond the bridge spanning the Afon Porthllwyd. Turn left and follow this lane W and S to a gate (0.8km) then turn right onto a path winding N then W.

The path continues uphill past a cottage to a wall stile (1.1km) on the left, touching the route of the Llanbedr walk.

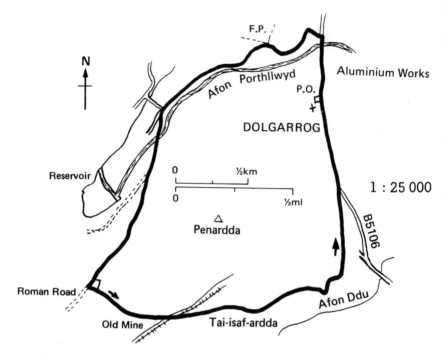

Continue south-westerly following the river bank past a waterfall (1.4km), through a fence opening to a stile (1.6km), and upstream through another fence opening (1.7km) to a stile by a council road (2.0km).

Turn left and follow the road S across a bridge which spans the river. After passing beneath a pipeline and crossing another bridge spanning a channel (2.4km) from the reservoir, take the wheeltracks bearing S to the top of the hill (3.4km, 2.1ml; elevation 382m, 1254ft). Ascending, one rises quickly above the reservoir and, looking back, there is a very good view of the lower Conwy Valley.

On the ridge, between Penardda to the NE and Moel Eilio to the SW, astride the route of a Roman road, take the left fork, bearing E then SE, down to a pipeline from Llyn Cowlyd. Continue over a footbridge, an old railway track and another footbridge spanning a stream and on, bearing 080°/090°, to a bridge spanning a channel from Cowlyd. On the descent there is an impressive view of Cowlyd, bearing 230°, gripped between the mountains of *Clogwyn Du* – black precipice, on the west side, and *Creigiau Gleision* – blue rocks, on the east.

Continue E along wheeltracks to the ruins of Tai-isaf-ardda – the lower houses of Ardda, site of a community dating back to medieval times. The medieval village of Ardda, and its field systems, covered an area of about 1000m from NE to SW and 500m from NW to SE. Abandonment began in the late eighteenth century but some residents remained until the 1920s.

Descending along the wheeltracks one has a view E across the valley of Plas Maenan and Cadair Ifan Goch, part of the walk from Llanddoged to Eglwysbach. Further down there is a gated opening in a stone wall on the left (5.6km, 3.5ml), from where the path winds northward down through the forest, joins a forest road (5.8km) for about 200m following it round a bend to the right, then turns sharp left continuing its northward course through the forest to stiles at 6.2km and 6.5km. We are now just behind the southern end of the village. Continue to the main road and Dolgarrog.

Trefriw

Here is a story of three waters: spring water, Conwy water and mountain water.

There is an old tradition in Trefriw which claims Nefydd Hardd, the twelfth-century founder of Gwynedd's Fifteen Nobel Tribes, as a resident of the Crafnant Valley. His descendants may have suggested the locality to Prince Llywelyn ap Iorwerth, monarch of Wales from 1194 to 1240, who lived in Trefriw and founded its church in order to spare his wife, Joan, daughter of King John, a steep climb to worship at Llanrhychwyn. Llywelyn the Great's residence here could be attributed to a medicinal quality in local waters – a discovery that may well have originated with the Romans a thousand years earlier.

Trefriw Chalybeate Wells were established in 1863 following discovery during the previous century, possibly dating from 1753, that water rising from a cave at the foot of *Allt Cae Coch* – hill of the red field – was impregnated with extraordinary quantities of iron and sulphur. A spa, offering mineral water as a curative and for bathing, transformed

Trefriw Village   *circa 1907*

Trefriw into a resort, with consequential effects upon transport in the Conwy Valley.

From Llandudno and Colwyn Bay, visitors to the Wells could enjoy a cruise by paddle steamer up the Conwy to Trefriw Quay. A suspension bridge (the Gower) was built across the Conwy to provide quick access from the railway station at Llanrwst to the Trefriw spa.

Who can explain the comings and goings of fashion? At any rate, the building that housed the pumproom remains. Presumably, mineral waters will continue to flow from the foot of Allt Cae Coch in the future as in ages past.

The waters of the Conwy offered Trefriw a different distinction – pearls. There is some doubt as to whether the

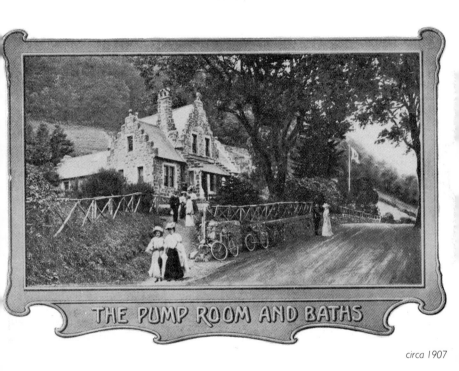

THE PUMP ROOM AND BATHS

circa 1907

Romans were the first discoverers but it is claimed that the Trefriw pearl fisheries were, in the nineteenth century, more productive than those nearer the mouth of the river. It is said that the large *horse-mussels* in which the pearls grow may still be found in the Trefriw area.

Tref means town, *rhiw*, hill. *Trefriw:* hilltown, or town by a hill. Certainly the steep grades behind Trefriw (pronounced Trĕvr-ōō) which Llywelyn's Joan found so tiring, endorses the aptness of this name. More important for the town's daily life is the unlimited supply of mountain water flowing down through lakes Crafnant and Geirionydd. This invaluable resource has been used in Trefriw since the Industrial Revolution for turning raw wool into cloth.

The Trefriw Woollen Mill is remarkable in encompassing an entire industrial and commercial process from purchase of raw wool to sale of finished product in the retail market; remarkable also in having achieved continuity over a period of nearly two hundred years from beginning as a *pandy* in the early nineteenth century; remarkable again in that its source of power has remained the ever-renewable, non-polluting water of the Afon Crafnant flowing from the two mountain lakes, Crafnant and Geirionydd.

About 1900 water wheels were replaced by hydro-electric turbines driven by a diversion from the river providing power from a net head of 130ft (43m) before being released back into the river and flowing on into the Conwy.

Originally, the mill serviced the needs of local farmers, processing part of their fleeces into cloth and blankets for the farmers' own use, and buying in the remainder. Now, the Snowdonia wool, noted for its hard-wearing qualities, is supplemented from other sources in order to impart softness, creating a quality of material suitable for weaving into an extensive range of textile.

Survival in a world of developing commercialisation seems to have been made possible by two conditions: production of quality products at competitive prices; dedication on the part of the family that have managed the mill since 1859, and by those who have invested their working lives in this thriving enterprise.

Walk 9

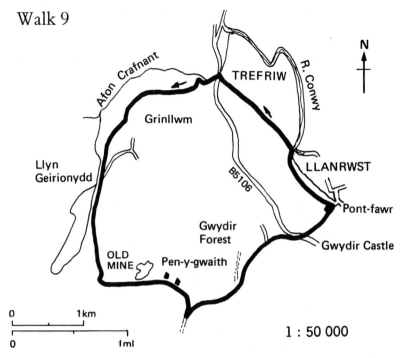

Trefriw – Geirionydd – Gwydir Forest – Llanrwst – Trefriw:
11.6km, 7¼ml.

From the main road bridge in front of the Trefriw Woollen Mill (00km; elevation 16m, 50ft) walk S for 100m along
the B5106, turn right by the school and 90m up the hill take
the left fork bearing SW. At the T junction (0.4km) turn left
for 100m, then right and continue SW up the wooded mountain path to critch-cratch 1.

Avoiding turnings-right, down to the valley bottom, follow the path round the mound of Grinllwm. *Crin*, or *grin*, is
dry, *llwm* bare. *Grinllwm:* dry and bare.

Continue to critch-cratch 2 and on to the northern end
of Llyn Geirionydd (2.9km, 1.8ml; elevation 197m, 600ft)
where the path joins a council road from Llanrhychwyn. Follow the road along the eastern shore of the lake to a gated
opening (3.3km; map ref: 765612) at the edge of a plantation.

Take the path, bearing S, which rises quickly up the hillside where one has a near aerial view of the lake. The path joins another from the left (3.7km) and continues, bearing 170°, to a footbridge (3.9km) and on to a stile at the boundary of old mine workings (4.2km, 2.6ml).

Walk round the mine to a stile 100m SE of the workings and follow the path E to a reservoir at the edge of a forest plantation.

From the southern shore of the reservoir (4.8km) follow the path across a forest road (5.0km), up through the plantation to a stile (5.2km) and across another forest road near the cottage Bwlch-y-gwynt. *Gwynt* is wind; *Bwlch-y-gwynt:* gap in the wind. The path continues, passing Pen-y-gwaith on the left, to a field gate opening on the right, down the hill, crossing a forest road (5.6km), by-passing an old mine (5.8km), and on down to a council road (6.1km, 3.8ml).

Turn sharp left along the road, continue NE to Nant Cottage (7.9km), on to the B5106 (8.5km) and Llanrwst. Before reaching the Llanrwst Bridge, turn left in front of *Tu-Hwnt-i'r-Bont* – the house beyond the bridge – dating from about 1480, once a courthouse, now a cafe and shop in the care of the National Trust.

Continuing NW from *Pont-fawr* (big bridge) and Tu-hwnt-i'r-Bont we pass the historic Llanrwst Church on the opposite bank. This stretch of water is one of the favoured spots of Conwy River anglers. It is also the site of many floods. That is why near the west bank there is an earth dyke – known as The Cob – incidentally providing an elevated river footpath extending beyond Trefriw.

Continue to the foot suspension bridge and tread the path of the nineteenth-century spa clients to Trefriw.

Betws-y-coed

A walker wanting to escape milling throngs of humanity at the height of a tourist season can easily satisfy his desire in Betws-y-coed. Humanity keeps to the main roads and the ever-enticing shops, restaurants and bars, only occasionally straying to glimpse a well-publicised view. A short distance away – up the slopes of the hills or along the river bank – nature's peace reigns: the deep peace of the forests attended by buzzing insects and chirping birds. The hum of rushing traffic along the valley roads soon fades as you penetrate this sanctuary.

A century of commercialisation has not ruined nature's design in Betws-y-coed. These hills are too intractable for that even if the Forestry Commission's dull green blanket has covered the slopes where sheep once grazed, and paths, once trodden, now lie beneath the spruce. Here are sculptured four river valleys: the tributaries Llugwy, Lledr and Machno, carved through the mountains to the mainstream Vale of Conwy. This grand junction of waterways has, not surprisingly, produced an interesting display in the art of bridge building ranging from pre-historic to modern.

From the railway station walk downstream 500m and you find the *Stepping Stones*, a ford where the Conwy can be crossed at low water. The modern alternative is Sapper's Bridge, behind the railway station, a foot suspension bridge built in 1930 to replace a bridge constructed by a company of army engineers during the First World War.

There is, of course, Thomas Telford's Waterloo Bridge across the Conwy, *Y Bont Haearn* – the Iron Bridge – as it is locally known, built in 1815 when the A5 was being established as the main route for the Irish Mail between London and Dublin.

A kilometre upstream from Telford's bridge, and just a few hundred metres downstream from the enchanting Fairy Glen, is the semi-circular stone arch of Beaver Bridge, or *Pont yr Afanc*, built about 1800. *Afanc* refers to a water monster which, according to legend, lived in the deep pool known as Llyn yr Afanc.

Right in the heart of the village, at the point where a community once lived on the banks of the Llugwy in isolated self-sufficiency, is *Pont-y-pair* – the bridge of the cauldron, referring to the frothy turbulence which this five-arch structure spans. Its construction date is not known but it is thought to be mid-fifteenth century.

About 1.3km upstream from Pont-y-pair is Miners' Bridge, a fascinating structure that is not so much a bridge as a ship's gangway allowing safe passage between the river's high northern bank and its lower southern bank. This is a very old crossing place, evidently once part of a Roman road from Dolwyddelan; but it acquired its name because lead miners used it in the nineteenth century as a short cut between the hamlet of Pentre-du and the pits north of Betws-y-coed. The last of the Betws-y-coed mines, Aberllyn, closed in 1904.

Over time, nature heals human intrusion into the earth: spreading vegetation upon mine workings, incorporating quarry heaps into its artistic design. Only art endures, and with it the subjects that art treats. Betws-y-coed's good fortune lies in its two hundred year role as an artists' model. What has attracted them?

Climb the hills and notice the multiplicity of greens: dark and heavy where the plantations are but light and translucent in the deciduous woods. This is terrain in which nature's mood can change from hour to hour. A bright sun, penetrating into deep pockets of shadow, is succeeded by overhanging cloud scowling down upon implacable mountains, drenching valleys in lightning storms; followed by a hazy sunlight filtering through shining wet leaves into cascading water. Watch a waterfall from on high, remote enough to see its role in the general theme, its white foam in striking contrast to green woods and grey-brown mountains. Follow the rebellious torrent beneath an arched stone bridge and it soon becomes a law-abiding flow, smiling sedately, while – if you are there in the right season – its salmon glint as they leap.

In the autumn topography is bathed in colour. This is often the most settled season and the time when one can see how much deciduous woodland there is, the trees spaced in natural pattern so that light penetrates the changing colours to the carpet of leaves on the forest floor.

Winter can be a time of unmuffled sounds, especially if one chooses a clear frosty day when the sun comes up like a blood-red ball in an infinite light blue sky. Now you can clearly hear the distant waterfall, swollen with soaking rains. Remark on the quiet and you will be heard across the valley. It is a time to breathe the purest of pure mountain air and feel the simple joy of living.

David Cox (1783–1859), probably the most celebrated of Betws-y-coed's itinerant artists, sought to assimilate these river valleys – with their cottages, meadows, water mills, mountains – into a sublime romanticism, always depicting humans as interacting within the landscape, representing a harmonious relationship with nature. Cox equated his artistic interpretation with a political philosophy: a good landscape being "in all its parts free and unconstrained" . . . which . . . "equally suits all free governments".

Who would deny that a capacity to sustain controversy in the second century following his death is not the least of an artist's accomplishments?

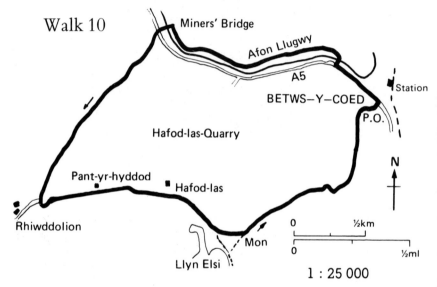

Betws-y-coed – Miners' Bridge – Rhiwddolion – Llyn Elsi – Betws-y-coed: 7.6km, 4.8ml.

From the Betws PO (00km; elevation 33m, 100ft) walk NW along the A5 to Pont-y-pair (0.4km), turn left after crossing the bridge and follow the path alongside the bank of the river to Miners' Bridge (2.0km). Descend to the southern bank, cross the A5 to the hamlet of Pentre-du and continue on a broad path, bearing SW, that was once a Roman road from Betws-y-coed to Dolwyddelan. The path crosses forest roads at 2.6km and 3.0km and then, 600m further on, forks right down to the deserted village of Rhiwddolion.

Rhiwddolion

At least until the fourth decade of the present century smallholders' wives carried their baskets of eggs and butter from this secluded hill village down the Roman road to market in Betws. Having disposed of their produce they would pack their baskets with provisions and trudge back up the path to their homes.

Rhiwddolion was a place where a man could rent a smallholding and at the same time earn a wage as a quarryman. Rising before five each morning the men would tramp along the Roman road to the railway station at Pont-y-pant and catch a train to Ffestiniog where work in the quarries started at seven. Returning home by six they had time, during the longer evenings, to do an hour's work in their fields before dark. In high summer many would be up by three to do a stint at harvesting before setting out for the quarries. This little community with its shop and chapel (the chapel served as a school on weekdays and a Sunday School on Sundays)

was eliminated by the great depression of the early 1930s which closed the Ffestiniog slate quarries. A local quarry, Hafod-las, had closed earlier in the century.

Returning to where the path forks 200m above the village (3.6km) take the left fork and follow the path eastward along the fence to a gated opening about 40m S of the cottage Pant-yr-hyddod (4.0km). *Pant* is a hollow, *hyddod* stag. *Pant-yr-hyddod:* stag hollow.

Continue E to a fence stile (4.4km), turn right along a forest road, take the left fork and follow left at the next fork 100m further on. Continue along the forest road, passing the deserted farmhouse Hafod-las (4.8km), for 300m to a point where the road veers left. Follow a path veering right, then left, to a monument at the northern end of Llyn Elsi (5.3km, 3.3ml; elevation 262m, 800ft). This quiet water set in a peaceful upland is a fisherman's paradise – even when the fish refuse to bite!

Follow the path eastward across two forest roads (5.8km and 6.1km) then NE and N down to the parish church, which dates from the fourteenth century, and to Betws.

Walk 11

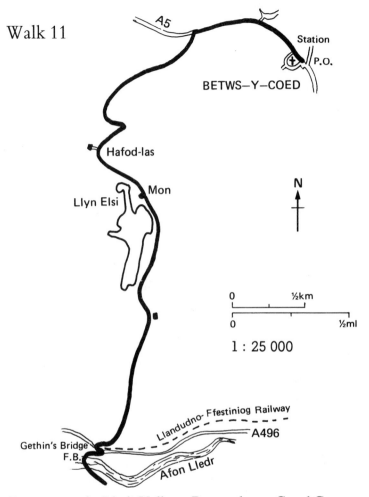

Betws-y-coed – Lledr Valley – Penmachno – Capel Garmon –
Betws-y-coed: 26.8km, 16.8ml.

Betws-y-coed – Penmachno: 12.7km, 7.9ml.

From the Betws PO (00km, elevation 33m, 100ft) follow
the A5 westward for 800m to a gated left-turning into the
forest. Continue S to SW along the forest road, avoiding
turnings at 1.0km and 1.2km. At 1.6km take the fork which

continues through a gated opening on a bearing of 240°, passing a barn (1.9km) on the left, and the deserted farmhouse, Hafod-las, on the right. Here we join the Rhiwddolion to Betws walk as far as Llyn Elsi.

Turn left along the forest road, 70m beyond the Hafod-las farmyard, and continue for 300m to a point where the road veers left. Follow a path veering right, then left, to a monument at the northern end of Llyn Elsi (2.8km, 1¾ml; elevation 262m, 800ft).

Continue along the eastern shore to the SE corner of the lake (3.6km; map ref: 783549), 30m east of the dam wall, where a path enters the forest on a bearing of 160°. Follow the path past a ruined cottage (3.9km), across a forest road (4.2km), and straight on down the stream path leading to Gethin's railway bridge (5.0km, 3.1ml).

This monumental structure was created by Owen Gethin

72

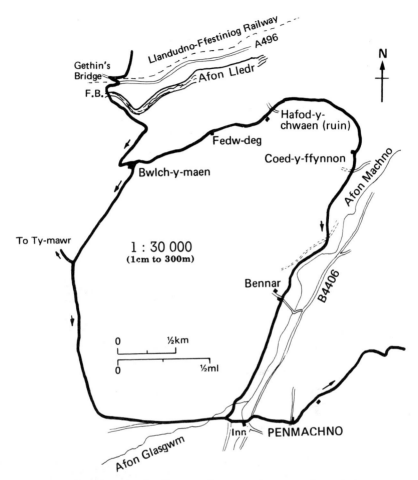

Jones (1816–83), the Penmachno engineer and poet, to carry the Llandudno–Ffestiniog line, one of the world's finest scenic railway routes, across the Lledr Valley. Construction commenced in 1875 and was completed in 1878. The weekly wage of a labourer on the construction site was six shillings; a mason received eight shillings a week.

Under the road arch and 70m east along the A496 there is a stone stile which lets one down into the enchanting world of the Lledr Valley. Follow the path W to an iron footbridge which spans the Afon Lledr; continue left, bearing 160°, to a wall opening (5.4km); left along wheeltracks through a gated

73

opening and over a bridge; and right, bearing 090° then 150°, up the hill to a forest road (5.9km). From the road continue uphill, bearing 230°, through mixed woodland to a stile (6.3km) and, 100m further on, follow the path round to E and on to the seventeenth-century farmhouse Bwlch-y-maen (6.7km, 4.2ml; elevation 213m, 650ft). *Bwlch* means gap, *maen* stone. *Bwlch-y-maen:* gap in the stone.

We now have a choice of route to Penmachno. For the western route continue S along the farm drive for 70m to a field gate opening on the right where a path bears 210° to the yard gate of a deserted cottage. Follow this path to a field gate opening by a forest road (7.3km), turn right along the forest road and continue to a council road (8.0km, 5ml).

Here a diversion may be made, of 800m (½ml) NW along the council road, to Ty Mawr, birthplace of Bishop William Morgan (1541–1604), translator of the Bible into Welsh. Published in 1588, the year in which England repelled the attempted invasion by Spain, the Welsh Bible may be observed as part of the struggle to avoid reversal of the Reformation, the central purpose of Europe's leading Catholic power. Granting Welsh speakers their own Bible helped secure independence from Continental domination. It was also a decisive event in ensuring survival of the Welsh language. Ty-mawr, now in the care of the National Trust, displays William Morgan's story and achievement.

Returning to the junction of the forest and council roads (8.0km), continue S along the council road and then eastward (9.3km) to Penmachno (11.2km, 7ml; elevation 164m, 500ft).

For the eastern route from Bwlch-y-maen (6.7km) follow a path from the eastern farmyard gate SE past a well and E up the hill to a fence stile (6.8km), through the woods and directly over a forest road (6.9km) to a stile at the edge of a field (7.1km). Cross the field (080°) to a gated opening leading to the sixteenth-century farmhouse Fedw-deg (7.3km). *Fedw* means birch; *deg*, or *teg*, fine. *Fedw-deg:* fine birch.

From the east gate follow the path eastward through field gate openings and along wheeltracks by the southern edge of the plantation. Continue eastward, passing the ruin of Hafod-y-chwaen (7.8km) on the right, to a fence stile (7.9km) on the left. Follow the path E/NE down through the plantation, across a forest road (8.0km) and on, passing a ruined cottage on the right.

The path descends through mainly deciduous forest and broadens out to wheeltrack width, winding E/SE then S to a gated opening (9.3km) where one looks out from the forest onto the Machno Valley. Continue SW to the sixteenth-century farmhouse Coed-y-ffynnon (9.5km, 5.9ml). *Coed* means trees, *ffynnon* well. *Coed-y-ffynnon:* trees of the well.

Follow the farm drive S/SW past an outbuilding to a forest road (9.8km). Cross the road and continue SW for 50m to a stile at the edge of the forest. The path winds SW to S down through the forest, descending to a forest road (10.3km). Cross the road to a field gate opening and follow wheeltracks SW to the bank of the Machno, then on through fields to the drive of the sixteenth-century farmhouse Bennar (11.2km).

Cross the farm drive to the field gate south of the barn and continue (210°) along the edge of the field to a stile where wheeltracks lead on to Penmachno (12.7km, 7.9ml).

Penmachno

Emerging from the forest into the Machno Valley one sees a village that was built of the rocks from its surrounding hills: the same kind of blue-grey stones that form the walls in Bishop Morgan's house, Ty Mawr, and the buttresses of Gethin's Bridge, just over the ridge in the Lledr Valley. One may think that Penmachno presents a perfect blend with its environment; but, looking at some of the houses now being built with the kind of machine-made blocks that are used everywhere, one can at least say that future observers will have no difficulty in deciding where economics drew a dividing line.

Stone is very much part of Penmachno's story which

takes us back to Stone Age people who worked flint in the
Glasgwm Valley, south-west of the village, and to Bronze
Age people who continued the practice of building cairns
over their graves well into early Christian times. In the
churchyard and nearby there are five early Christian tomb-
stones, one of which describes a person as lying *"in hoc
congeries lapidum"* – in this heap of stones. Another men-
tions the mid-sixth century Consul Justinus; and another, of
the fifth or sixth century, refers to Vendotia, the Latin name
for Gwynedd.

Penmachno literally describes the head of the Machno
which is one of the Conwy's main tributaries. The river rises
five miles upstream above Cwm Penmachno, a small settlement at the end of the valley, surrounded by its derelict slate
quarries, walled-in by the mountains of Ffestiniog with its
end-of-the-world reputation still intact. Downstream at the
centre of Penmachno itself is Pont Llan, spanning the Afon
Machno with five flattened elliptical arches. The bridge was
re-built in 1785 for a cost of £200.

Sixteenth and seventeenth-century farmhouses are scattered over a fairly wide area of the locality. Some have been noted already on the walk over from the Lledr Valley. Solidly built, with very thick stone walls, huge fireplaces, oak beams and curved stone lintels, most of them still function as working farmhouses, giving an impression of what life was like for those living in this part of Wales three or four hundred years ago.

	map ref:	period:
Ty Mawr	770524	16c
Bwlch-y-maen	782531	17c
Fedw-deg	789533	16c
Coed-y-ffynnon	804530	16c
Bennar	794518	16c
Hafod-dwyryd, with barn and outbuilding	790499	17c
Pen-y-bryn, with barn	787503	17c
Blaen-y-glasgwm (uchaf/isaf)	766495	16c
Pen-y-bedw (uchaf/isaf)	780484	17c
Dugoed	806522	16c
Dulasau-isaf	822526	16c

Penmachno – Capel Garmon: 10.4km, 6.5ml.

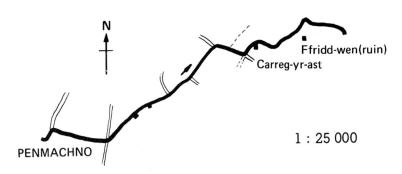

N

Ffridd-wen(ruin)
Carreg-yr-ast

1 : 25 000

PENMACHNO

From the Machno Inn (12.7km) walk E along the B4406 for 60m and turn right along the path to critch-cratch 1 (13.1km) and critch-cratch 2 by a council road (13.2km). Cross the road and veer left to a gated opening near a cottage (13.4km), then continue to a deserted cottage Rhos-y-maen (13.6km). The path veers right through wall openings, past a ruined cottage and on to wheeltracks leading down to a gated opening (14.3km). Turn right to a field gate and follow the farm drive to Carreg-yr-ast (14.7km, 9.2ml; elevation 262m, 800ft).

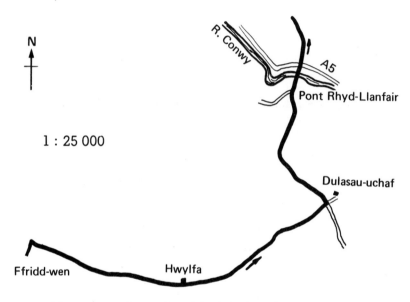

From a gated opening SE of the farmhouse follow a path that crosses a stream and wanders NE to the ruin of *Ffridd-wen* – white sheepwalk. Continue past the ruin for 100m and, after crossing a stream, follow right, bearing E/SE, upstream to a wall opening (15.8km). Bear 100° across moorland pasture, a habitat of grouse, to a wall opening on the rise to a summit, then continue to the ruin of Hwylfa (16.3km, 10.2ml; elevation 360m, 1100ft). From this high point we have a good view S and SE.

Follow wheeltracks E to a fence opening and on, bearing

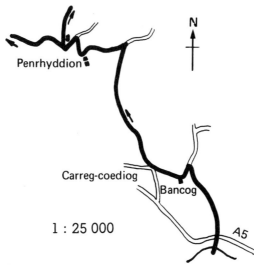

Penrhyddion

Carreg-coediog

Bancog

A5

N

1 : 25 000

080°/070°/060°, to a council road opposite a farm drive leading to Dulasau-uchaf. Turn left along the road and continue NW then N to Pont Rhyd-Llanfair (map ref: 828524; 18.5km, 11.6ml). This single-arched bridge with a span of 27m (90ft) is thought to be the work of Robert Griffiths of Tan-yr-allt in the Lledr Valley, who succeeded, after two attempts had failed, in building this present fine arch across the Conwy in 1780.

Cross the A5 and follow the council road northward for 600m. Take a sharp left turn into the Bancog farm drive and right from the farmyard gate to Carreg-coediog (19.5km). *Carreg* is stone, *coediog* wooded. *Carreg-coediog:* wooded stone. Pass to the rear of the farm buildings, turn right onto a farm road, bearing 350° then 320°, and on to a field gate opening and critch-cratch 3. Continue up the field to a gated hedge opening and across the next field to a farm drive. Turn left and follow the drive W to the *Penrhyddion* – free tops – farms, past *Pella* – farthest – to *Canol* – middle (21.0km, 13.1ml; elevation 230m, 700ft). We now have a choice of route.

To continue directly to Betws-y-coed, follow the drive westward for a further 400m to a gated opening. Leave the drive and continue to the right along wheeltracks, bearing

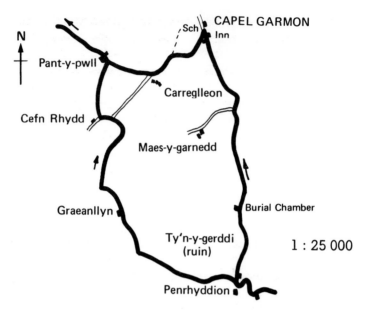

N

CAPEL GARMON

Sch Inn

Pant-y-pwll

Carreglleon

Cefn Rhydd

Maes-y-garnedd

Graeanllyn

Burial Chamber

Ty'n-y-gerddi
(ruin)

1 : 25 000

Penrhyddion

290°, past the ruin of *Ty'n-y-gerddi* – house in gardens, on the right, and *Graeanllyn* – gravel pit, on the left, to a TV mast (22.5km, 14.0ml). Follow the path to the right, bearing 030°, then N and NW, to the farm drive of Cefn Rhydd. *Cefn* is a ridge, *rhydd* free. *Cefn Rhydd:* free ridge. Turn left along the drive and continue towards the farmhouse for 100m, then right, bearing N, for 150m to a wall stile. Follow the path N to NE, joining the path from Capel Garmon on the right, and continuing to Pant-y-pwll (23.5km, 14.7ml). *Pant* is a hollow, *pwll* a pool. *Pant-y-pwll:* hollow pool.

To proceed to Capel Garmon from Penrhyddion-canol bear N opposite the house, through the barnyard to a gated opening near the farmhouse Penrhyddion-uchaf. Follow wheeltracks winding northward through open woodland for approximately 300m, then left, bearing 330°, down to critch-cratch 4. Continue N for 100m to critch-cratch 5 at the boundary of the ancient burial chamber: "a monument erected in the Neolithic Age 2500–1900BC for the communal burial of the dead." One of the few remains left by the first cultivators of this land.

From critch-cratch 6, northward across the field, pass to the right of the farmhouse, Ty'n-y-coed, through a field gate opening, and follow the path round the base of the hill to critch-cratch 7, across the field to critch-cratch 8 and the Maes-y-garnedd farm drive. *Maes* is field, *garnedd* tumulus. *Maes-y-garnedd:* field of the tumulus. Turn right along the drive and left along the council road for 500m to Capel Garmon (23.1km, 14.4ml; elevation 228m, 750ft).

Capel Garmon

If a straight line were drawn from Llanrwst to Ysbyty-Ifan the centre point of the line would fall upon Capel Garmon. In the days when sheep and cattle were driven overland this hill village formed part of a droving network connecting the lower Conwy Valley with a droving road from the Lleyn Peninsula through Ffestiniog to England. Capel Garmon was one day's droving from Llanrwst's market. Ysbyty-Ifan was reached on the following day. When approaching up these hills something of the welcoming aspect that must have greeted those earlier travellers can still be felt. The narrow crooked village street, the cosy inn and bakery opposite: one feels thankful that steep hills and narrow roads have helped to preserve the character of this place.

Capel Garmon – Betws-y-coed: 3.7km, 2.3ml.

From the White Horse Inn continue N for 100m to critch-cratch 9, on the left opposite the school, follow the path along the churchyard wall to a fence stile, then down the hill to another fence stile by a council road (23.4km). Turn right and follow the road westward for 500m to a wall gate opposite the north entrance to the farmhouse Carreglleon. Continue across the field (290°) to a wall stile and on to Pant-y-pwll (24.2km, 15.1ml).

Pass between the house and the barn and along the drive for 100m, follow left over a stone stile to critch-cratch 10, and

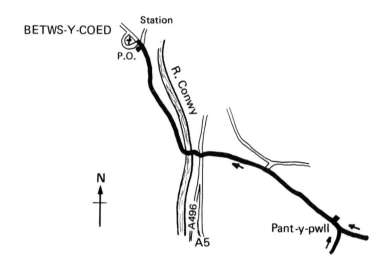

on (320°) to a gated opening. Continue to wheeltracks, turn
left to a gated opening, and right bearing 310°, to a wall
opening. Follow the path downhill to the drive of a caravan
park, turn left for 40m, then right and continue (310°) down
through the woods to Betws-y-coed.

Ysbyty-Ifan

Standing near the junction of the village road with the
B4407 (map ref: 84174883) one can visualise Ysbyty-Ifan as it
was before the Second World War. Here is a mill with its
wheel still in place, a pair of cottages, a wheelwright's joinery
shop, a smithy – all silent now but providing a vision of the
days when the village was alive with work and purpose; when
farms needed men and horses, and people found most of
their supplies locally. Those who worked away from the village – in the slate quarries of Ffestiniog, for example – would
start their weekends by tramping across the mountains to
their homes; for this was a place that people came back to; a

village of singers, chapel societies – and especially legendary hospitality, a tradition that can be traced back to Ysbyty-Ifan's founding.

According to Archdeacon Thomas who wrote a history of the diocese, an extract from which is displayed in the church, a hospital (or hospice) was established here, about the year 1190, by Ifan ap Rhys. *Ysbyty* means hospital. The hospital stood to the west of the present church on ground which once served as a village green but is now built over. Ifan obtained for his hospital the privilege of a sanctuary which meant that travellers could find here safety from pursuit – even from authority. It was a refuge and resting place for any traveller in these wild mountains. During the time of Llywelyn the Great the sanctuary was apparently extended to take in most of the valley including the area of Llyn Conwy. The hospitallers were called knights rather than monks but they were responsible for performing divine services and administering sacraments.

Not surprisingly the sanctuary was increasingly abused as the religious fervour which supported its foundation waned. During the fifteenth century it became a shelter for bandits who plundered the area with impunity until they were eliminated by Meredith ap Ieuan, founder of the house of Gwydir.

The privilege of the sanctuary was withdrawn in Tudor times, after the dissolution of the monastries, but Ysbyty-Ifan's reputation has continued, as shown by the words of the bard, Dafydd Nanmor, who described a certain man's hospitality as: "ei groeso fel croeso Ysbyty-Ifan": his welcome was the welcome of Ysbyty-Ifan.

Also unchanged is the wild landscape: peat moorland and rocky summits with only a few sheep here and there as far as the eye can see.

Walk 12

Ysbyty-Ifan – Llyn Conwy, the source of the River Conwy –
– Ysbyty-Ifan: 19.6km, 12.2ml.

Ysbyty-Ifan – Llyn Conwy: 7.4km, 4.6ml.

From the Ysbyty PO (00km; elevation 216m, 710ft) cross the hump-backed bridge that spans the Conwy and continue to the B4407. Turn left and 40m up the hill turn right along a lane which leads to a grass path (0.5km). Continue westward uphill through field gate openings to a farm road (0.9km). Turn left along the road for 60m to a field gate opening on the right, then continue W/SW up the hill, along the line of the grass path, through a field gate opening (1.2km) and on to the ridge (1.7km, 1.1ml; elevation 412m, 1350ft).

Here the mound of *Foel-ddu* – black top – but in late summer covered with purple heather, bears 230°, the line of our route. Continue to a wall gate at the base of Foel-ddu,

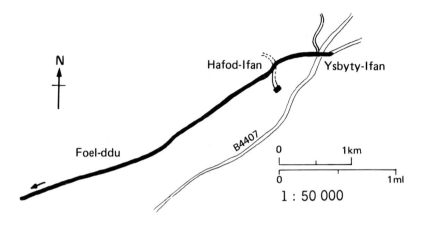

N

Hafod-Ifan

Ysbyty-Ifan

Foel-ddu

B4407

0   1km

0   1ml

1 : 50 000

and up to the summit (3.1km, 1.9ml; elevation 459m, 1508ft) where there is a splendid full-circle panoramic view of the whole surrounding area. To the west the line of our walk to Llyn Conwy crosses a trackless terrain of rough pasture. Across the valley to the south the profile of the return route to Ysbyty-Ifan is hung on the peaks of Bryn-mawr 210°, Moel Trwyn-swch 200° and Ffridd-y-fedw 145°.

From Foel-ddu we set a course of 250° and follow it across a succession of ridges. It is as well to check the bearing and fix a point with the eye on each ridge. A pine plantation on the right is a landmark: one should keep at least a km (about ½ml) from it. Llyn Conwy does not come into view until we climb the ridge south of the plantation. Here we should be heading for the centre of the lake which resembles the shape of Africa. Approaching the SE shore we may note three tiny islands one of which was the breeding haunt of great black-backed gulls until they were exterminated in 1890 in punishment for their preying upon the nests of local grouse. We make for the southern tip – the cape end, the source of the Conwy (7.4km, 4.5ml; elevation 457m, 1500ft).

But where is the source of the Conwy? Where is the significant outward flow giving legitimate birth to our river? One searches but there is nothing to be seen – except beneath

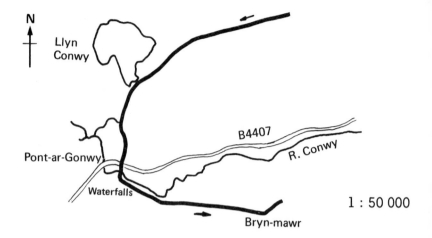

a line of rushes where there is a rather uncertain trickle that could surely have no pretension of embellishing itself with a name and bestowing it upon an area of the country.

A couple of hundred metres south along the metalled road the heart lifts to a singing gurgle from the pebbles of the stream-bed. Four hundred metres further on a gentle stream, a full metre wide and accommodating the contributions of several streamlets from the moor, now flows beneath the feet. Leaving it flowing out to the moor to gather further strength we continue southward to the B4407 (8.9km).

Cross the road and follow a path S for 200m. Here we observe a genuine river, heavy with peat brought down from the moor by countless tributary streams, flowing with confidence over a succession of waterfalls (elevation 426m, 1400ft). Cross the waterfalls and follow the Conwy's southern bank, bearing 110°, for about 700m to a point where the river winds NE.

Bear E to the summit of Bryn-mawr (map ref: 802443; 11.7km, 7.3ml; elevation 515m, 1680ft). We now stand on the highest point of the walk. Foel-ddu across the valley, as well as Moel Trwyn-swch and Ffridd-y-fedw on the line of our route ahead, are below us.

Continue on 060° to the summit of Moel Trwyn-swch

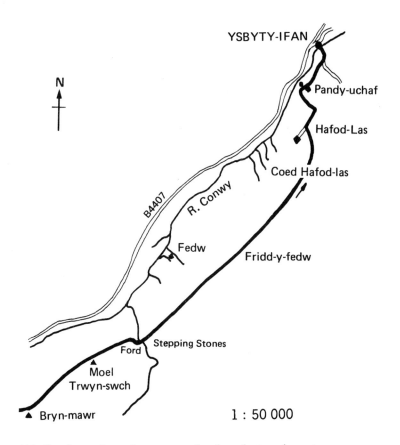

(12.6km), and on down to a ford and stepping stones across the ample tributary Afon Serw.

Here it is necessary to change bearing slightly, from 060° to 050°, to make directly for the summit of Ffridd-y-fedw (16.1km, 10ml) where the way down to Ysbyty-Ifan can be seen. Keeping well below and to the left of the next summit, Penffridd-sarn, skirt the wood, Coed Hafod-las, on the left, and continue along the contour of the hill to an opening in the walled boundary of the farm Hafod-las. Follow wheel-tracks across fields and through wall openings to the farm road (18.0km) which leads down to the farmhouse Pandy-uchaf (18.7km) and then on to Ysbyty-Ifan.

The Conwy Valley Way

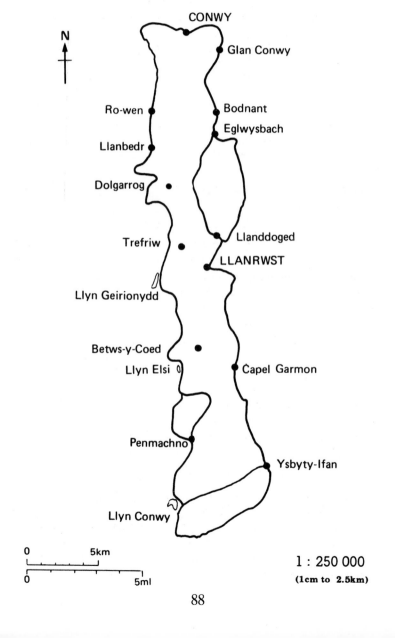

N

CONWY
Glan Conwy
Ro-wen
Bodnant
Eglwysbach
Llanbedr
Dolgarrog
Trefriw
Llanddoged
LLANRWST
Llyn Geirionydd
Betws-y-Coed
Llyn Elsi
Capel Garmon
Penmachno
Ysbyty-Ifan
Llyn Conwy

0   5km

0   5ml

1 : 250 000

(1cm to 2.5km)

The Conwy Valley Way

These twelve circular walks provide raw material for charting a long-distance circular walk round the entire Conwy Valley. We shall begin in Llanrwst which is the centre or, as some would say, the "capital" of the Conwy Valley.

Llanrwst – Eglwysbach: 14.4km, 9ml.

Use the first part of Walk 1 from Llanrwst (00km) to Pen-bryn-doget (2.4km). Here we join Walk 2 but we have a choice of route. We may use either the first part of Walk 2 in reverse: Pen-bryn-doget – Pantllin-mawr – Waen-oer – Gwern-bwys – Pennant-uchaf – Bryngwian – Goleugell – Eglwysbach; or, continue down the hill to Llanddoged (3.2km) and use the second part of Walk 2 from Llanddoged to Eglwysbach.

Eglwysbach – Conwy: 13.7km, 8.6ml.

From the Bee Inn, Eglwysbach (00km), use the first part of Walk 3 from Eglwysbach to Bodnant (2.7km). From the Garden entrance walk N along the council road to the A496 (3.6km), continue northward along the main road to Croesau farmhouse (4.1km), fork left along a council road, left again at Waenynyd (4.4km) and follow the farm road to Ty'n-y-coed (5.2km). Continue northward along a field path to Trallwyn (5.7km), up the farm drive to a council road, fork right then left and follow the road to Beswick Nursery (6.6km). Turn left and follow a field path northward, crossing a farm road (7.5km), to Bryn Gower (7.8km). Turn right along the council road and continue to Glan Conwy (9.0km), on through Llandudno Junction and across the estuary to Conwy.

Conwy – Ro-wen: 12.7km, 8ml.

From Lancaster Square, Conwy (00km), use the first part of Walk 5 over Conwy Mountain to Sychnant Pass (4.3km). Continue SE but at the top of the descent, which takes us past the cottage Pen-y-bwlch, fork right (5.3km) along wheeltracks, then left, and continue southward passing Waen-y-fedwen (5.9km), Llechan-uchaf (6.6km), Hendy

(6.9km), Glynnog (7.8km), Tan-yr-allt Henryd (8.9km), Tyddyn-mawr (10.1km), Ty'n-y-coed (10.9km), Coed-mawr (11.8km) and down to Ro-wen.

Ro-wen – Llanbedr-y-cennin: 3.3km, 2.1ml.

From the Ty Gwyn, Ro-wen (00km), set out as for Walk 6 but continue past Glasgoed (0.4km) to Gorswen (1.0km). Turn right alongside the barn and follow the path S and SE across fields and streams to Tyddyn-y-bluen (1.8km) and on to Llanbedr.

Llanbedr – Miners' Bridge, Betws-y-coed: 24km, 15ml.

Use Walk 7 from the Bull Inn, Llanbedr (00km), to Rowlyn-isaf and down past Llidiard Fadog but turn right onto Walk 8 where the two walks coincide (4.8km). Continue on Walk 8 to the site of the ruined village of Ardda. From the ruin at the NE end (9.5km) bear S through a wall opening and continue down through the forest to an iron footbridge which spans the Afon Ddu (9.9km). Turn right over the stile and continue up the hill to wheeltracks near the ruin of Tyddyn Wilym. Turn left and follow the wheeltracks bearing E, then SE and S, past Gelli Newydd (13.4km) to a path bearing 210° along a cemetery wall. Follow the path to the Crafnant road (14.3km), turn right, cross the Afon Crafnant opposite Gymannog (14.6km), continue SW along the farm road to a path on the left (15.1km) and up the hill to join the route of Walk 9 (15.5km). On reaching the disused mine workings (19.5km) east of Llyn Geirionydd continue S along the mine road then SE to Miners' Bridge, Betws-y-coed.

Betws-y-coed – Pemachno: 13.2km, 8¼ml.

From Miners' Bridge (00km) use Walk 10 to Rhiwddolion and Llyn Elsi (3.3km) where we join Walk 11. Continue across the Lledr Valley to Gethin's Bridge (5.5km) and Bwlch-y-maen (7.2km) where we have a choice of route, westward by way of Ty Mawr or eastward by way of Coed-y-ffynnon, to Penmachno.

Penmachno – Conwy source – Ysbyty-Ifan: 18km, 11.2ml.

From the Machno Inn, Penmachno (00km), take the village road SW along the southern bank of the Afon Machno and continue to Hafod-dwyryd (0.7km, map ref: 790499) an impressive farmhouse dating from the seventeenth century. From the back of an outbuilding at the rear of the house follow wheeltracks SW across the Afon Oernant (1.3km) and on to another seventeenth-century farmhouse, Pen-y-bedw (2.8km, map ref: 780484). Climb S to the Pen-y-bedw summit (4.3km; elevation 526m, 1730ft) where there is a splendid view of the Machno Valley and the surrounding terrain. Continue SE and S to the southern tip of the lake: the source of the Conwy (5.8km).

From the source we may use either part of Walk 12 to reach Ysbyty-Ifan.

Ysbyty-Ifan – Llanrwst: 20.3km, 12.7ml.

From Ysbyty-Ifan PO (00km) rejoin Walk 11 N/NW along the council road at the entrance to Dylasau-uchaf (3.5km) and continue to Pont Rhyd-Lanfair (4.7km) and Capel Garmon (9.3km). Take the side road opposite the Capel Garmon Church to a field path that wanders N and NE offering splendid views down the Conwy Valley. On reaching a farm road (10.2km) turn right and continue to Bryn-rhyd (10.8km). Follow the farm road northward past Nant-isaf (12.9km) but instead of turning left to a council road turn right (N) on a path which descends to a ford (13.8km); continue to Oaklands (14.3km), on past Plas-tirion (15.2km) and NE along a farm track to the B5427. Turn left and continue along the road for 700m to a path on the right bearing E to a footbridge (16.8km) and the village of Melin-y-coed (17.1km). Turn right over the bridge in the centre of the village and continue N along the Carmel road to a stile on the left 100m beyond Bryndyffryn (18.0km). Follow the path as it winds westward to a stile-ladder (18.7km), descend to wheeltracks and continue downhill (SW) for 100m to a stile on the right where a path leads westward down to a stream and continues alongside a school boundary to Llanrwst.

Total Distance: 120km, 75ml.

Flora and Fauna in the Conwy Valley

Those fortunate enough to walk in the Conwy Valley in spring or early summer can enjoy not only the new season's debut of every variety of deciduous tree that grows in Britain, but also a wide selection of wild flowers. The Eglwysbach Branch of the Women's Institute recorded in their Scrapbook for 1965 a list of plants collected on one farm by Mr Bernard Salt, a local resident. The list includes:

Basil-thyme, Hedge Bedstraw, Bell-heather, Larger Bindweed, Greater and Slender Birdsfoot Trefoil, Buddleia, White Campion, Common Cow-wheat, Long-stalked Cranesbill, Clustered Dock, Fat Hen, Feverfew, Foxglove, Fumitory, Golden-rod, Grass Poly, Groundsel, Common Hemp-nettle, Hop, Black Knapweed, Ling, Common Mallow, Marjoram, Sickle Medick, Corn Mint, Monkshood, Mugwort, Stinging Nettle, Pineapple Weed, Scarlet Pimpernel, Polygonum, Round-headed Rampion, Rose Bay, Wood Sage, Devil's-bit Scabious, Field Scabious, Sheep's-bit, Lesser Spearwort, Spiked Speedwell, Ploughman's Spikenard, Yellow Stonecrop, Sun Spurge, Thrift, Common Toadflax, Traveller's Joy, Red Valerian, Common Vetch, Violet, Yarrow.

The Conwy Valley has a fairly equable climate including a rainfall that varies from 70cm (28 inches) at sea level to 140cm+ (55 inches+) on the higher ground where, besides a profusion of heaths and heathers, one may be fortunate enough to observe these interesting plants:

the meat-eating *Sundew* whose leaves are covered with long sticky hairs which curve inwards to trap insects;

the *Bogbean* which is good for both cattle and humans for if the leaves are boiled the water is said to alleviate rheumatism;

the *March Marigold* a gay yellow flower with large, dark green shiny leaves;

the *Bilberry* with its pinkish flowers and edible black berries;

the *Cranberry* which produces pink flowers and edible white berries spotted red or brown.

Hedges in the Conwy Valley are among the finest in Britain. Usually tall and well trimmed one often feels that a hedge concentrates the plant life of the countryside, as well as providing living quarters for fauna. Stand before a hedge and, without moving the head to right or left, see how many different plants you can identify. Here is one example:

ash, blackberry, blue bell, campion, chestnut, elderberry, hawthorn, hazelnut, holly, honeysuckle, ivy, oak, primrose, wild rhubarb, speedwell, wild strawberry, sycamore, vetch, violet.

Mammals. Most of the wild British varieties are represented. The *badger* is well known for the controversy it has caused between farming interests and conservationalists. *Rabbits* are less plentiful than *hares*. *Foxes* are thought to be less common than they used to be. *Stoats, weasels, voles* and *hedgehogs* are numerous. Both the *red* and *grey squirrel* survive here. In addition, the Forestry Commission claims the *polecat* and the *otter*.

Reptiles include *adders, grass snakes, smooth snakes,* and *slow worms*.

Bird life is profuse and the following, with Welsh names in brackets, are among the more distinctive Conwy Valley species:

buzzard (bod), curlew (gylfinir), grouse (grugiar), hawk (hebog), kestrel (cudyll), peewit or lapwing (cornchwiglen), partridge (petrisen), pheasant (ffesant), wild duck (hwyaden wyllt), woodcock (cyffylog), woodpecker (cnocell-y-coed).

Fish life. It is said that when the first *sparling* appears in the Conwy winter is over. Why this small fish should choose the Conwy, alone of all Welsh rivers, to bring tidings of longer and warmer days is not known. It is netted in the lower reaches during two or three weeks in March and then it vanishes leaving the river to better known species.

The *trout* season lasts from 1st March to 30th September. Even the smaller tributaries and mountain streams offer keen sportsmen a chance to land trout. This can sometimes be done, especially after a flooding rain, by "tickling" for trout which may be sheltering beneath an overhanging rock or bank, and then taking the fish by hand. As trout are apt to take on the colour of their surroundings those in the higher streams tend to be darker if the stream drains peaty terrain.

Salmon are returning to the Conwy in greater numbers than for many years. Now, one may again see salmon leaping up the cascades and waterfalls of the Llugwy and Lledr as well as in the main river. The season lasts from 1st April to 17th October: the period of the year when the adrenalin of Conwy Valley salmon anglers flows in anticipation of landing fish heavier than ten pounds.

Picture Locations

Front Cover: Fairy Glen
where the Conwy generates
enchanting turbulence

page 60:   Trefriw
a resort in Edwardian elegance

page 61:   Trefriw Spa
a site for discriminating tastes

Back Cover: The Conwy Valley
flanked by the mountain stronghold
with its Snowdonia Peaks

Bibliography

Wyn, Sir John, *The History of the Gwydir Family*.

Halhed, W. B., *Archeological Research in the Nant Conwy District and Neighbourhood*, 1902–10.

Elias, T., *History and Associations of the Abbeys and Convents of the Vale of Conwy and District*, 1912.

Williams, W., *Ancient and Historic Llanrwst*, 1930.

Rowlands, E. D., *Dyffryn Conwy a'r Creuddyn*, 1947.

Davies, Rev. Ellis, *Pre-historic and Romans Remains of Denbighshire*.

Denbighshire Historical Society Transactions, 23 volumes.

Jones, Frank Price, *Crwydro Gorllewin Dinbych*.

An Inventory of the Ancient Monuments in Caernarvonshire, Volume 1: East, 1956, H.M.S.O.

Morris, John Lloyd, *Hunangofiant Gwerinwr*, 1972.

Senior, M., *Portrait of North Wales*, 1973, Hale, London.

Roberts, S. Tudur, Ysgol Eglwysbach 1835–1985.

Wildman, S., Lockett, R., Murdoch, J., *David Cox 1783–1859*, Birmingham Museums and Art Gallery 1983.

Trefriw Chalybeate Wells, 1908.

Ordnance Survey Publications.

Acknowledgments

I pay my respects to the oral historians, whose recollections about some of the sixteen towns and villages which lie on these circular walking routes, I am pleased to record; among whom are:

> Mrs Jane Evans (*Nain*), Llanrwst
> William Bleddyn Lloyd, Dolwyddelan
> David Evans, Llanrwst and Rhiwddolion
> Durham Priddle-Higson, Llanddoged
> Bob Hughes, Llanrwst.

Also to: Martin Puddle, Head Gardener of Bodnant Gardens
The Librarians of Gwynedd County Library Service

By no means least to: Alwena, for reading, researching and evaluating the script.